A Comparative Study
of the *Beowulf* and the *Aeneid*

London : Humphrey Milford
Oxford University Press

A
Comparative Study of
the *Beowulf* and the *Aeneid*

By Tom Burns Haber

Phaeton Press

New York

1968

Originally Published 1931
Reprinted 1968

Library of Congress Catalogue Card Number — 68-29338
Published by PHAETON PRESS

To My Best Teachers
My Father and My Mother

Preface

*A*BOUT *four years ago, without any hope of return beyond the pleasure of the adventure, I began writing out a translation of the* Aeneid. *Before this project was half finished, I undertook in a more serious way a study of the* Beowulf, *finishing a written translation of it simultaneously with the completion of the translation of the Latin epic. In turning from one poem to the other, I often made note of resemblances of style and construction, which in time, as instances began to multiply and fall into a semblance of order, left the impression that these analogies in the* Beowulf *might be more than merely fortuitous.*

The question at length suggested itself: What evidence is there that the Latin epic might have contributed to the composition of the Beowulf? *A natural extension of my reading discovered that this question had been raised and possible bases of comparison pointed out by not a few scholars in the field of Old English. This present study represents an attempt to collect and arrange the results of these discussions, and a following-out of the various clews which they suggested.*

It is impossible to prove conclusively that the Beowulf *at any place shows traces of the influence of the* Aeneid. *I have constantly kept in mind that the nature of the problem more often requires balancing probabilities than attempting to state conclusions. It is believed, however, that an analysis of the Old English epic which points out the resemblances which it bears to the* Aeneid *is in itself valuable; and that the cumulative effect of these examples will establish the strong prob-*

ability that there is indeed a closer connection between the two poems than has heretofore been credited; even though it must always be admitted that any specific point referred to may find its explanation in unadulterated Germanic tradition.

From the first this study has received the supervision of Dr. G. H. McKnight of the English department, Ohio State University; and to him my sincerest thanks are due. I wish also to acknowledge my indebtedness to Professor Marbury B. Ogle of the Department of Latin and Professor Hans Kurath of the Department of German.

I have used Klaeber's text of the Beowulf *(New York, 1922) and the text of Paul Lejay (with some minor variations in spelling) for the* Aeneid *(Paris, 1926).*

Contents

Chapter I

Introduction: Survey of Opinion

IT IS not a new theory that Vergil's *Aeneid* may have had something to do in the composition of the Old English epic *Beowulf*. Among the earliest attempts to show a relationship between the two poems was a study by Georg Zappert, *Virgils Fortleben im Mittelalter* (Vienna, 1851), which by an exhaustive list of parallel quotations traced Vergilian echoes through the *Beowulf* and other epic literature of the Middle Ages. A careful survey of the popularity of Vergil in northern Europe formed the introduction of Zappert's work. In the most important recent book dealing with the Old English epic, Professor W. W. Lawrence's *Beowulf and Epic Tradition*, occur these statements:

"We do not know whether any Germanic poem of the epic amplitude of *Beowulf* existed before the introduction of Christianity. It is quite possible that none did exist, and that the plan and general execution of the whole was suggested by Vergil or other classical models,—in short, that *Beowulf*, like the *Aeneid*, is a book-epic."[1]

"It has frequently been suggested that the new learning in Britain may be seen reflected in *Beowulf* in the influence of the *Aeneid*. This is supported not so much by parallelisms of phraseology and incident, which, though sometimes striking, are not sufficiently close to be conclusive as evidences of borrowing, as by the great popularity that the *Aeneid* enjoyed among those acquainted with Latin letters. Both the Irish and the Roman ecclesiastics in northern Britain knew it well; in-

[1] pp. 10-11.

deed, of all the great works of classical antiquity it was one of the best known and least misunderstood in the early Middle Ages. It would surely have appealed to a poet versed in Germanic tradition, on account of its plot, its heroic temper, and its detailed information in regard to a long-past age. The state of society and the ideals of the warrior class which it sets forth are very similar to those that existed among Germanic peoples at the time of the invasion of Britain. . . . So, then, while the influence of Vergil may be regarded as entirely possible, it can not be conclusively established."[2]

W. P. Ker in *The Dark Ages* points to the size and dignity of the style of the *Beowulf* as evidence that into its makeup went something more than was inherent in the generating influences that produced the other Old English literature. He states that what we know of the antecedents and development of the early English epic indicates that in the *Beowulf* "this comparatively well-filled narrative poetry may not be an independent product of the English or Teutonic genius. There is too much education in *Beowulf*, and it may be that the larger kind of heroic poem was attained in England only through the example of Latin narrative. The English epic is possibly due to Virgil and Statius; possibly to Juvencus and other Christian poets, to the authors studied by Aldhelm and Bede."[3]

R. W. Chambers in his work *Beowulf, An Introduction*, raises the question: "Are we to suppose any direct connection between the classical and the Old English epic?"[4] He reminds us that the similarities in the poetry of nations passing through their Heroic Age may be accounted for by social backgrounds more or less similar, out of which heroic lays and epics were born. "But," he continues, "there is much more in *Beowulf* than mere accidental coincidences of phrase or situation." Like the *Aeneid*, the *Beowulf* is not merely a tale told

[2] Lawrence, *Beowulf and Epic Tradition*, pp. 284-5.
[3] *The Dark Ages*, pp. 251-2.   [4] pp. 329 *ff.*

by a "simple-minded romancer" about a hero's doings from the cradle to the grave. The heroes are thrown into critical situations in foreign courts, where their former exploits are related by the actors themselves. The songs of the minstrels are not only mentioned but their contents are set forth. Mr. Chambers, for the sake of showing what seems to be verbal similarity, quotes the well-known speech of Jove to Hercules (*Aeneid* X, 467-9) and Beowulf's words to Hrothgar (1386-9).

Though Chambers sympathizes with Chadwick's opinion that a writer knowing Vergil would have expressed his knowledge of the *Aeneid* more openly in a vernacular poem, the fact that he does not do so, in Mr. Chambers' opinion, must not be considered as proof that the Latin epic should be ruled out of consideration as a possible model for the Old English epic. He suggests that the feeling of the modern reader that the author of the *Beowulf*, if he indeed knew the *Aeneid*, would have left more definite traces of his sources "rests largely upon the analogy of other races and ages. Is it borne out," he continues, "by such known facts as we can gather about this period? The reticence of *Beowulf* with reference to Christianity does not harmonize with one's preconceived ideas."

It is quite beyond the intention of this study to *prove* that the *Beowulf*-poet imitated Vergil or used the *Aeneid* as a source for his epic. The limits of such an investigation as this were well defined by Professor Klaeber in his two contributions in *Archiv* CXXVI.[5] The introduction states that "Ob in irgendwelchen der genannten Punkte eine direkte Einwirkung des römischen Epos stattgefunden hat, oder ob etwa schon vorhandene Richtungen nur verstärkt wurden, oder ob alle Analogien nur auf Zufall, d.h. auf Ähnlichkeit der Verhält-

[5] pp. 40 *ff.*, 339 *ff.*

nisse und Umstände beruhen, lässt sich nicht mathematisch entscheiden."[6]

This study is an attempt to follow out and bring to a conclusion as definite as possible several lines of investigation proposed by a number of critics examining the two epics from various points of view. The most that the present writer can hope for is that he may establish the strong probability that there is in the *Beowulf* evidence that the author did possess an acquaintance with the *Aeneid* and took from it various plot-motifs, stylistic devices, and turns of expression which appear in the Anglo-Saxon epic. It will be shown that the *Beowulf* in many details is out of harmony with the literature of which it is chronologically a part, and that not infrequently it leaves the impression of departing significantly from the traditions of the people among whom it arose. An attempt will be made to show that some of these broader inconsistencies may find explanation in references to the *Aeneid*. Other stylistic peculiarities in the Old English poem will be seen to have a precedent in Latin style, often specifically in Vergil's epic. As a necessary introduction, an examination will be made of the popularity of Vergil in Britain about the end of the seventh century.

[6] *Archiv* CXXVI, p. 44.

Chapter II

The Popularity of Vergil in Britain About the End of the Seventh Century

ON page xxiv of Papillon and Haigh's introduction to their edition of Vergil (Oxford, 1892) it is stated that (excepting the New Testament) the works of Vergil had "a more rapid multiplication and more careful preservation of MS. copies" than was enjoyed by any other author whose compositions were transmitted to the Middle Ages. There were many reasons for the popularity of the Latin poet: the respect in which he was held by the churchmen; the prestige his name wielded among grammarians and rhetoricians; and the ambition of many of the barbarian conquerors to trace their ancestry back to the fabulous kings of early Rome. Independent of Vergil's moral teaching, the high regard the medieval writers and readers had for his style and diction set his name above all other masters of poetic form.

Influence of the Church. To the churchmen of medieval Europe Vergil was the divine pagan, the prophet of the Messiah, the foreteller of the reign of peace on earth. The scanty details of the poet's life required no great adornment of tradition to transmit him to the Middle Ages in a character singularly noble, abstemious, and devout. Many were the hours spent in the pious effort to reconcile Christian doctrine with the sentiments of this pre-Christian poet, this Roman Isaiah. Vergil's significant phrase *Non, mihi si linguae centum oraque centum*, etc., (VI, 625) was easily turned from its original purpose of hinting at the terrors of hell to praising the glories of the Christian God. So Alcuin used *Semper honos nomenque tuum laudesque manebunt* (I, 609).[1] From the *Aeneid* as well as from the writing of Saint Paul, the medieval monk might take a text for his musings; and it was regarded as a labor to a particular degree meritorious to show that the texts were more alike than different, that they were inspired by the same spirit. Phrases such as these must have come ready to the pen and tongue of the literary ecclesiastic: *mens sibi conscia recti* (I, 604); *auri sacra fames* (III, 57); *improbe amor, quid non mortalia pectora cogis* (IV, 412); *auri caecus amore* (I, 349); *unum pro multis dabitur caput* (V, 815), etc. Zappert says of classical allusions found in the writings of the clergy that, unless there is definite proof that the author had access to another poet, the natural conclusion is that Vergil is the most probable source.[2] Vergil even became in the hands of the zealous Christian a power to combat heresy and condemn paganism out of the mouth of the divine pagan himself. To quote Zappert again:[3] "Die Bekenner Christi, in des Nöthigung gesetzt, den Federangriffen ihrer Widersacher polemisch entgegen zu treten, ergriffen die in derartigen Fehden bewährte Defensiv-Offensiv. Sie bekämpften den heidnischen Feind mit seinen eigenen Waffen, und bewiesen ihm aus seinem so hochgepriesenen Virgil nicht nur die Nichtigkeit

[1] Zappert, *Virgils Fortleben im Mittelalter*, p. 22.

[2] So lange daher nicht der Beweis gegeben, dass der Clerus des Mittelalters mit einem andern Dichter eben so vertrauten Umgang als mit dem unseren gepflogen, so lange wird bei classichen Ähnlichkeiten und Anklängen Virgil die Vermuthung der Vaterschaft für sich haben. (*Virgils Fortleben im Mittelalter*, p. 6.) Zappert quotes (p. 16) this statement from the unedited works of Abelard, which may be taken as a general statement of the opinion of the medieval monk upon the *Aeneid*: "Ex laboribus Aeneae tolerantiae exemplum habemus; ex affectu eius in Anchisem et Ascanium, pietatis; ex veneratione, quem Diis exhibebat, ex oraculis quae poscebat, ex sacrificiis quae offerebat, ex votis et precibus quas fundebat, quodammodo ad religionem incitamur; per immoderatum vero Didonis amorem ab illicitorum appetitu revocamur."

[3] *ibid.*, p. 4.

des Polytheismus, sondern selbst die Wahrheit eines einigen Gottes. Mehr noch, Verse der vierter Ecloge wurden messianisch und Virgil, der Sänger des Aeneas, zu einem Seher Christi gedeutet; in welcher Prophetenrolle wir ihn auch in den Mysterien des Mittelalters auftreten sehen."

In Britain the same problems were debated by the men of the church, and a justification or compromise was usually the result of their admiration for the beauties of Vergil and their detestation of the paganism with which he was associated. Herbert, Bishop of Norwich, tells of Christ appearing to him in a dream, saying: "I know that from your youth till now you have served in the sacerdotal office; but why do you keep with you the lies of Ovid and the fictions of Vergil? It is not fitting that the same mouth should preach Christ and recite Ovid."[4] In spite of dreams, however, and the more substantial reproofs from the heads of the Church, the medieval monk undoubtedly found it difficult to eradicate from his memory the poems which had been an integral part of his education and which perhaps furnished the only relief to the somber round of the life of cell and cloister. Countless quotations from the letters of ecclesiastics of all ranks show how great an influence Vergil really possessed during the Middle Ages in Britain.

The spread of classical learning kept even pace with the spread of Christianity in England. The Anglo-Saxons had been little affected by the establishment of the faith during the fourth and fifth centuries. Saint Augustine's mission in 597 was much more influential, beginning in Kent and extending the doctrines of Rome by means of missionary activity in the north. In Northumbria, particularly, as Bede relates, the new faith struck firm root. Following the example of Saint Patrick, the Irish missionaries, who represented the acme of the

---

[4] See Comparetti, *Vergil in the Middle Ages*, p. 92.

learning of the day, had been active in North Britain up to the middle of the seventh century,[5] when the influence of the Irish church was definitely eclipsed at the Synod of Whitby (664) by the power of the Roman organization. This was an additional guarantee of the perpetuation in Britain of all that ancient Rome had bequeathed to the Middle Ages, and assured a much greater circulation of classical manuscripts than would have been possible under the rule of Saint Patrick.[6] The new acquaintance with classical literature consequent upon the drawing together of the bond between Britain and Rome did not stifle the interest of the educated classes in the old vernacular lays. In fact, to quote Gummere[7]: "It established a neutral ground on which classics and barbarism could in some manner join hands and so save what was best in each." "The Teutonic chief," says Chambers,[8] "often had a larger mind than the modern student. . . . I love to think of these incongruities: to remember that the warrior Alfred, surrounded by *thegn* and *gesith*, listening to the 'Saxon songs' that he loved, was yet the same Alfred who painfully translated Gregory's *Pastoral Care*."

Latinists like Aldhelm and Bede were not ashamed to try their hand at native verse, and Alfred the Great had native tales told to his children in the tongue of their Teutonic fore-

[5] For a discussion of early education in Ireland see Douglas Hyde's *A Literary History of Ireland* (London, 1920), Chap. XVII, "The First Schools of Christian Ireland," and Roger's *L'Enseignement des Lettres Classiques d'Ausone à Alcuin*, Chaps. VI, VII. See also Jubainville's *Littérature Celtique* (Paris, 1883), Vol. I, Chap. IX, "Les Écoles d'Irlande au sixième, au septième, et au huitième siècle." The latter, speaking of Armagh (and other monasteries founded in the fifth century) says in part: "Alors furent créés les principaux des grands monastères d'Irlande, centres littéraires en même temps que religieux d'où un essaim d'apôtres rapporta, dans diverses régions du continent et dans la Grande-Bretagne redevenues barbares et restées en partie païennes, le culte des lettres classiques et l'enseignement théologique du christianisme." (p. 370.)

[6] See Lawrence, *Beowulf and Epic Tradition*, pp. 7, 271-3.

[7] *Germanic Origins*, p. 9.   [8] *Beowulf, An Introduction*, p. 121.

fathers. Both Alfred and Malmesbury bear testimony to Aldhelm's proficiency as a public singer;[9] the latter says that "to
instruct the people" Aldhelm was wont to take his place upon
the public bridge and recite and compose songs of matter both
sacred and profane, in Latin and in the vernacular. Saint
Boniface (680-754), the apostle to Germany, studied at Ex-
eter and at Nutcell, near Winchester. He undoubtedly became familiar with Vergil during his education in Britain; in
his *Aenigmata* he echoes line 568 of the Seventh *Aeneid*. Saint
Boniface writes *et poenas Erebi lustrent per devia Ditis*. This
is reminiscent of *hic specus horrendum et saevi spiracula Ditis/
monstrantur.* (*Aeneid* VII, 568-9.)[10] Zappert comments that
the vernacular sagas arose in spinning-rooms, taverns, and
similar places of public concourse. The taverns were resorted
to quite frequently in the ceremonies of marriage, christening,
etc., upon which occasions the services of the clergy were of
course required. Thus the officiating men of the church would
become familiar with native songs in native language. More-
over, if Zappert is correct, they sang and learned them; "In-
dividuen dieses Standes [des Clerus] erscheinen nicht bloss
als Zuhörer volksthümlichen Gesanges, sondern üben solchen
sogar selbst. Geistliche fixiren historischen Volksliedern ent-
nommene Stoffe in ihren lateinisch geschriebenen Geschichts-
werken."[11] This last sentence shows how free must have been
the interchange of material from the vernacular to the Latin.
There were both civil and ecclesiastical laws against the practice of the clergy to write vernacular songs, as there were laws
which prohibited them to eat or drink in the taverns with the
laity. The fact that these restrictions became more numerous

---

[9] "Nativae quoque linguae non negligebat carmina; adeo ut . . . nulla unquam
aetate par ei fuerit quispiam, poesim Anglicam posse facere, tantum com-
ponere, eadem apposite vel canere, vel dicere. Denique commemorat Elfredus
carmen triviale, quod adhuc vulgo cantitatur, Aldhelmus fecisse." Zappert,
Virgils Fortleben im Mittelalter, p. 27, quoted from an early *Biographia*.
[10] See Zappert's *Virgils Fortleben im Mittelalter*, p. 22.   [11] *ibid.*, p. 6.

and obligatory from the seventh century on may bear the interpretation that many of the clergy were in the habit of mingling freely in the common life of the people, thus bridging the gap between Latin and native English.[12]

It is in this early period of the union with the Roman church, the time when, to quote Chambers, "the chasm between secular poetry and ecclesiastical learning was more easily bridged" that the *Beowulf*-poet composed his epic. The church Latin that he knew was not creative; its purposes were instruction and adornment. He found the poetic impulse in the Teutonic life of the Britain of two centuries previous; thence were his materials drawn in the form, probably, of scattered lays and little epics. He undoubtedly had to deal with an *embarras de richesse*, so far as the substance of his poem was concerned. Ready to his hand, doubtless an integral part of his poetic equipment, was Vergil's great epic, to provide him with a model in as many ways as he cared to or was able to use it.

Following the Synod of Whitby, Theodore of Tarsus, the primate of England, brought about amicable relations between the hostile kingdoms of Northumbria and Mercia, and made possible a reign of peace which lasted for thirty-five years. This period was particularly favorable to literary activity: Theodore himself was a distinguished scholar, active in founding schools and extending the benefits of classical learning; King Aldfrith of Northumbria (685-705) had studied in Ireland[13] and had attained some skill in writing Irish verse. It was Northumbria that profited chiefly by the labors of the indefatigable Benedict Biscop, who made no less than six journeys to Rome (the last about 686), returning each time with treasures of books, sacred and profane. In return

---

[12] For a discussion of the same condition in Ireland see Jubainville, *Littérature Celtique*, Vol. I, pp. 385-90.

[13] See Douglas Hyde's *A Literary History of Ireland*, pp. 221 *ff*.

for his activity he was liberally rewarded by special favors from the Northumbrian monarchs—not only Aldfrith, but Ecgfrith, his predecessor.

Aldfrith attracted to his court a company of literary men, chief among whom was Aldhelm (*c.* 650-709). There is little doubt that Aldhelm was acquainted with all the works of Vergil.[14] His treatise on metrics (*Liber de Septenario et de Metris, Aenigmatibus, ac Pedum Regulis*) contains nearly as many quotations from Vergil as all other Latin authors taken in sum. His evident familiarity with long passages of the *Aeneid* (the description of Fama, for instance, which he quotes in one of his Riddles) indicates that he must have had direct access to the Latin poet.[15] His poem *De Laudibus Virginitatis* reveals a number of Vergilian tags, which show an unmistakable preference for the words of the author of the *Aeneid*. Such phrases in his verse as *caelestibus armis, fama super aethera notus, cornua cantu, stipante caterva, limina portae, quo non praestantior alter,* etc., carry one as surely back to Vergil as "To be or not to be" makes one think of Shakespeare. Aldhelm quotes literally line 641 of the Seventh *Aeneid*: *Pandite nunc Helicona, deae, cantusque movete.* In his two verses *Facundum constat quondam cecinisse poetam/*

---

[14] Before Aldhelm, evidence of knowledge of Vergil is to be found in the Book of Gildas the Wise (*c.* 516-73) in which he echoes with peculiar appropriateness line 24 of the Ninth *Aeneid* (*multa deos orans, oneravitque aethera votis*), in his *De Excidio*, 25: "ut dicitur: innumeris onerantes aethera votis." He also makes reference to II, 120 (*obstipuere animi*, etc.) and II, 497 (*oppositasque evicit gurgite moles*). "Gelido per ossa tremore currente" (*De Excidio*, 6) may derive from *gelidusque per ima cucurrit / ossa tremor* (II *Aeneid* 120.) (See Sandys, *A History of Classical Scholarship*, p. 446.) The writings of the Irish monk, Columban (543-615), "include reminiscences of Sallust, Vergil, Horace, Ovid, and Persius." (*ibid.*, p. 452.) Zappert calls attention to the two following quotations from Columban's writings: *Somnus abest oculis, illum sonus excitat omnis*—(*nunc omnes terrent aurae, sonus excitat omnis*, II, 728) and *Nec trepido tales volvit sub pectore curas*—(*et veteris Fauni volvit sub pectore sortem*, VII, 254).

[15] See E. A. Savage, *Old English Libraries*, p. 29.

quo Deus et quo dura vocat fortuna, sequamur Zappert sees
an echo of lines 22-23 of the Fifth *Aeneid*: *Superat quoniam
fortuna, sequamur,/ quoque vocat, vertamus iter.* Aldhelm is
quoting directly line 677 of the Twelfth *Aeneid*: *Quo Deus
et quo dura vocat Fortuna, sequamur.*[16] Looking back through
his technical works, Aldhelm refers thus to his borrowing from
Vergil: "*Haec . . . collecta, quamvis mihi conscius sum illud
me Vergilianum posse jactare.*" His treatise on Latin poetry
sent to King Aldfrith contains numerous quotations from the
Aeneid; Aldhelm remarks that he is the first man in Britain
to acquire a comprehensive knowledge of the classics, and
urges the king not to neglect his books.[17]

Bede (673-735) shows less devotion to Vergil, although
his letters and more notably his *De Arte Metrica* contain
many Vergilian quotations. The oft-quoted couplet in his
hymn in honor of Queen Ethelrida gives evidence of Bede's
withdrawal from profane learning:

> *Bella Maro resonet, nos pacis dona canamus;*
> *munera nos Christi, bella Maro resonet.*
>
> —*Eccl. Hist.*, Book IV, Chap. 20.

Discussing the types of drama in the *De Arte Metrica*, Bede
compares Vergil's *Eclogues* with the dramatic portions of the
Holy Scriptures. The Book of Job is compared with the
Aeneid and the *Iliad* and the *Odyssey*.[18] The *Ecclesiastical
History* and many of Bede's minor poems reveal the author's
preference for Vergilian phrases. One finds in the *History* the
famous first line of the second book of the *Aeneid*: *Conticuere
omnes intentique ora tenebant;* neither can one mistake the
source of such phrases as *inque dies, haec ubi dicta, instau-
rat honorem, nec me sententia fallit,* etc. Zappert[19] quotes

[16] See Zappert, *Virgils Fortleben im Mittelalter*, p. 21.
[17] See further, Roger, *L'Enseignement des Lettres Classiques d'Ausone à Alcuin*,
pp. 288-303.
[18] See Baldwin, *Mediaeval Rhetoric and Poetic*, p. 132.
[19] *Virgils Fortleben im Mittelalter*, p. 22.

the following lines from Bede's *Life of Saint Cuthbert* and adjoins the Vergilian originals: *Obsequium sibi ferre rogans. Cui talia reddit*—(*dixerat. Aeneas contra cui talia reddit*, X, 530); *Frigora quoque volans percurrit sidera nimbus*—(*ignea rima micans percurrit lumine nimbos*, VIII, 392); *Expandit geminas supplex ad sidera palmas*—(*palmas nequiquam ad sidera tendunt*, V. 256) [cf. also *duplices cum voce manus ad sidera tendit*, X, 667]; *At revoluta dies noctis cum pelleret umbras*—(*et interea revoluta ruebat/ matura iam luce dies, noctemque fugarat*, X, 256-7). Bede's treatment of the story of the fall of Troy and the wanderings of Aeneas in his *De Temporibus* and *De Temporum Ratione* proves that he regarded these events as historic facts. All of the numerous quotations in Bede's last-named work are, without exception, taken from Vergil; and the author presumably considered his readers so familiar with the source of them that he did not take the trouble to name Vergil as the author. Some of the verses are merely introduced by such phrases as *et Poeta describens, meminit horum et Poeta, de qua Poeta,* etc. For men like Bede, Vergil was truly The Poet; he needed no other designation.[20]

Alcuin (*c.* 735-804), according to his own confession, had been in his youth *Vergilii amplius quam psalmorum amator.* In later life his love for his poetic master changed to hatred. In the preface to his commentary on the Song of Solomon he wrote:

Haec rogo menti tuae iuvenis mandare memento,
carmina sunt nimium falsi haec meliora Maronis,

[20] See Sandys, *A History of Classical Scholarship,* p. 468 and Roger, *L'Enseignement des Lettres Classiques d'Ausone à Alcuin,* pp. 304-10. Bede had been a pupil of Benedict Biscop, who probably inspired his love of collecting books. Bede also carried into Britain many books from the continent. (See G. F. Browne, *The Venerable Bede,* p. 7.)

haec tibi vera canunt vitae praecepta perennis,
auribus ille tuis male frivola falsa sonabit.[21]

He wrote and spoke against "the lies of Vergil," and, according to the anonymous *Life* (Chapter X), instructed his pupils
not to contaminate themselves with "the voluptuous eloquence of Vergil."[22] It is fair to suppose, however, that
Alcuin's changed attitude must be laid to his zeal for the
Church, which caused this open revulsion of feeling against
the beloved poet of his student days. It was natural that he
should, as a defender of the faith, require his pupils to read
nothing but the writings of the church fathers. Similarly he
asks, *"Quid Hinieldus cum Christo?"* and consigns that
"damned heathen" to eternal punishment. That his indigna-
tion against Vergil did not extend so far is proved by the
fact that, although he exhorted Riculf to prefer the Four
Gospels to the Twelve *Aeneids*, he (Alcuin) quoted Vergil in
his letters as late as 801.[23] Like many another devout church-
man in a like case, Alcuin takes refuge in the example of
Saint Paul, who *aurum sapientiae, in stercore poetarum in-
ventum, in divitias ecclesiasticae transtulit prudentiae; sicut
omnes sancti doctores, eius exemplo eruditi, fecerunt.* (Epistle
147.) Alcuin's verse contains more recollections from Vergil
than the poetry of Bede or Aldhelm can show; and in his
scholarly works, his *Grammar, Rhetoric, Logic*, etc., Vergilian
quotations outnumber the total of all other excerpts by a ratio
of more than four to one.[24] In his preference for Vergil in his

[21] Quoted in Comparetti, *Vergil in the Middle Ages*, p. 91.

[22] Legerat isdem vir Domini liberos juvenis antiquorum Philosophorum,
Vergiliique mendacia, quae nolebat jam ipse nec audire, neque discipulos suos
legere, "sufficiunt," inquens, "divini poetae vobis nec egetis luxuriosa sermonis
Vergilii vos polluifacundia." From the anonymous *Life*, quoted by Zappert,
Virgils Fortleben im Mittelalter, p. 32.

[23] See Gaskoin, *Alcuin: His Life and Work*, p. 191. Gaskoin believes that the
anonymous biographer's account of Alcuin's forbidding the study of Vergil
to his pupils is "possibly only a figment of the fertile monastic imagination."

[24] See Lorentz, *The Life of Alcuin*, pp. 26-9.

poetic works, Alcuin was doubtless following the universal practice of his times. In regard to this imitation and borrowing Zappert notes: "Die poetische Latinität zudem erscheint so vorwiegend eine Maronische, dass wir auf wenige Versificatoren stossen, an deren Zeilen wir nicht den Einfluss ihres Meisters nachzuweisen vermöchten."[25] Aside from literal quotations, Zappert calls attention[26] to the following imitations: *O quibus est semper bellorum vivida virtus*—(*bello vivida virtus*, V, 754); [cf. also *vivida bello/ dextra*, X, 609-10; *vivida virtus*, XI, 386]; *Ingreditur, heros veterum condignus avorum*—(*descendam, magnorum haud umquam indignus avorum*, XII, 649).

It is the estimate of O. M. Long[27] that references to Vergil in the letters of Alcuin outnumber all other quotations combined by more than two to one. Of deliberately quoted passages Long counts 81. His opinion is that Alcuin's quotations from the Latin poet are not so often for the sake of the moral as for pure embellishment of style—indicating that, whatever he said about "the voluptuous eloquence of Vergil," he never forsook his admiration of him. Sandys reminds us, too, that "the library at Berne possesses a MS. of Vergil in Caroline minuscules, which is believed to be either written in Alcuin's hand, or at least transcribed from his own copy, and which certainly once belonged to his monastery at Tours."[28] Commenting on Alcuin's verses to his brothers at York, Sandys says[29] truly that there is in them no prejudice against Vergil:

Moenibus Euboricae habitans tu sacra iuventus,
fas idcirco, reor, comprendere plectra Maronis,

[25] *Virgils Fortleben im Mittelalter*, p. 6.
[26] *ibid.*, p. 22.
[27] "The Attitude of Alcuin Toward Vergil," *Gildersleeve Studies*, pp. 381 ff.
[28] *A History of Classical Scholarship*, p. 476.
[29] *ibid.*, p. 477.

somnigeras subito te nunc excire Camenas,
carminibusque sacris naves implere Fresonum.[30]

Rhetoricians, Grammarians. Since Latin was the language
of the Church, and since the Church was the sponsor of education, Latin was necessarily in the curriculum of every medieval student. Grammar, taken in its largest sense, constituted
a predominant element in Latin study. The grammar-texts
most commonly used, in the words of one writer, gave the
appearance of Vergilian centos, so numerous were the quotations from this master of form. Taylor says, "Vergil was no
longer Vergil, but incarnate grammar and authoritative history."[31] It has already been pointed out that Vergilian quotations had an outstanding place in the technical works of
Aldhelm, Bede, and Alcuin. Zappert made a comparative
study of six of the most popular rhetorics in use during the
Middle Ages, to find that the number of quoted passages from
the three most revered Latin poets were in this proportion:
Vergil, 2,803; Horace, 250; Ovid, 105.

The Chroniclers. The legendary founders of Rome were
pressed into service by the barbarian rulers of the Middle
Ages, who pretended to derive their kingship from the imperial line of the state they overthrew. In the words of Zappert,
"Die Völker, unter deren eisernem Tritte das Reich des

---

[30] Alcuin's lines (1546-1553) from *De Pontificibus et Sanctis Ecclesiae Ebor-
acensis Carmen* may be quoted here. He is giving a list of the authors whose
works are to be found in his monastery at York:

> Quidquid et Althelmus docuit, quid Beda magister,
> quae Victorinus scripsere Boethius atque,
> historici veteres, Pompeius, Plinius, ipse
> acer Aristoteles, rhetor quique Tullius ingens.
> Quid quoque Sedulius, vel quid canit ipse Juvencus,
> Alcimus et Clemens, Prosper, Paulinus, Arator,
> quid Fortunatus, vel quid Lactantius edunt.
> Quae Maro Virgilius, Statius, Lucanus et auctor.

> —Reprinted from *The Historians of the Church of York and
> Its Archbishops,* Master of the Rolls Publications, 1879.

[31] *Classical Heritage of the Middle Ages,* p. 3.

Romulus in Stücken ging, mit Ebenbürtigkeits-Brüstung ihr barbarisches Reis auf trojanischen Edelstamm pfropfen."[32] This attempt at surrounding the early Teutonic kingdoms with something of the glory that was Rome must have had a powerful influence in extending the study of Vergil.

It is not easy to determine how early the Brutus-legend arose in Britain. Toward the end of the century in which the *Beowulf* may have been composed, Nennius describes the coming of Brutus (the grandson of Aeneas) to the island, which received from him the name *Britannia* (*et vocatum est nomen eius Bruto*.[33] Nennius mentions in his *Prologue* the sources which he professes to employ; the Brutus-tradition he may have derived from some of these ancient monuments. It seems reasonable to believe that the legend had been current in Britain for some time prior to the eighth century, though its beginning cannot be satisfactorily determined for our present purpose. Commenting on Nennius' statement of his derivation of his information about Brutus from "the ancient books of our ancestors," Giles says: "This proves the tradition of Brutus to be older than Geoffrey or Tyssilio, unless these notices of Brutus have been interpolated in the original work of Nennius." Tyssilio flourished about the year 600.

According to Fletcher,[34] Geoffrey was the first historian to tell of Hengist's stratagem of obtaining ground for a castle by the bull's-hide trick. This is probably a Vergilian borrowing. (See *Aeneid* I, 365-8.) How early the classical story became engrafted to British legend, it is impossible to say.

There is a hint of the blending of Teutonic and Roman sovereignty in the oldest English poem, *Widsith*. Here the order of descent is reversed: the barbarian does not derive from the Roman, but Caesar is made "a son of Woden"—to

[32] *Virgils Fortleben im Mittelalter*, p. 4.
[33] See Giles, *Old English Chronicles*, pp. 388-9, 391.
[34] *Arthurian Material in the Chronicles*, p. 61.

use Zappert's words. These are the words in question: *Cāsere wēold Crēacum ond Cǽlic Finnum* (*Widsith*, line 25).[35] Gummere's translation of the line is "Caesar ruled Greeks and Gaelic Finns."[36]

APPENDIX TO CHAPTER TWO

The Question of Homeric Influence. Homer has been studied as a source nearer akin than Vergil to the *Beowulf*. Chambers remarks that "It has been urged, as a *reductio ad absurdum* of the view which would connect *Beowulf* with Vergil, that the relation to the *Odyssey* is more obvious than that to the *Aeneid*."[37] There is no doubt that Greek was known in Britain at the time of the composition of the *Beowulf*, and Irish scholars had known it long before; but in comparison with Latin manuscripts, Greek manuscripts must have been extremely rare. M. R. James says upon this point, "The area in which Greek MSS. were produced in the medieval period was (with negligible exceptions) confined to Greece proper."[38] He says further[39]: "It is a temptation, when one turns to England, to enlarge upon the early history of Greek scholarship, but it is a temptation which must be resisted." The real starting-point for Greek learning in England, James continues, is with George Neville, Archbishop of York, who died 1476. The note of a scribe on a MS. of Demosthenes (now in Leyden) tells that he worked under the direction of Archbishop Neville and finished the MS. in 1472. In accord with these views is the opinion of A. F. West: "It is true that Theodore of Tarsus had brought in the teaching of Greek at York, and that Irish influence was favorable to Greek studies, so that there were probably Greek books in the York library. But

---

[35] See Chambers' *Widsith*, p. 192.
[36] *Oldest English Epic*, p. 193.
[37] *Beowulf, An Introduction*, p. 329.
[38] *The Wanderings and Homes of Manuscripts*, p. 12.
[39] *ibid.*, p. 16.

Alcuin, though he may have been acquainted with Greek sufficiently to read it a little, confined his own activities to Latin. Accordingly, though Aristotle and some of the Greek fathers appear in his catalogue, it is more likely that he is thinking only of Latin versions."[40]

Vergil, therefore, would seem entitled to claim more plausible consideration than Homer as being the source of the embellishments which the author of the *Beowulf* attempted to introduce into his poem. It can hardly be believed that a poet capable of producing a work as pretentious as the *Beowulf* would not have been familiar with the Latin poet whose influence we have seen to be so outstanding, not only in the literary activity of eighth century Britain, but in many other fields as well. Indeed, one would be much more inclined to believe that Vergil was known to the *Beowulf*-poet than to attempt to explain how the Old English writer could have failed to come into contact with and be impressed by the author of the *Aeneid*. This is posing a choice between probabilities; but in the light of the best evidence available, the weight of probability seems to point to Vergil as the chief extraneous influence in the Anglo-Saxon epos.[41]

[40] *Alcuin and the Rise of the Christian Schools*, pp. 36-7.
[41] Roger makes numerous allusions to the limited extent of the early study of Greek in Britain. See his *L'Enseignement des Lettres Classiques d'Ausone à Alcuin*, pp. 205-6; 268-72; 388-91.

Chapter III

Indications of Non-Germanic Influence in the *Beowulf*

THERE are in the *Beowulf* many elements which not only have no kinship with the other poetry of the age in which it was produced, but which show decided conflict with literary convention and historical fact, so far as we are able to attribute these standards to the Britain of the early eighth century. These isolating factors are of various kinds; many of them, not admitting of explanation as examples of poetic license, seem to indicate definite extra-vernacular influence. Furthermore, these inconsistencies appear to be more than incidental attachments to the poem; they are to be found, for instance, in the broader social background built up in the poem, as well as in numerous stylistic devices: all of which elements tend to distinguish the *Beowulf* from the genius of the language of which it is the greatest early monument.

G. A. Smithson in his study *The Old English Christian Epic* has shown that the use of episodic material, digressions, repetition, etc., definitely sets the *Beowulf* apart from the other Old English epics in the matter of plot-technique. He points out the fact that, whereas in the Christian epics (*Juliana, Elene, Andreas, Christ*), direct discourse is a main factor in advancing the plot, in the *Beowulf* it is very unimportant, though it occupies about two-thirds of the poem.[1] The speeches in the *Beowulf* are less realistic, more formal, than those of

[1] p. 367.

the Christian poems; this is a common epic quality, and provides another link between the *Beowulf* and epic poetry in
general. The Christian epics often sacrifice epic dignity to
emotional effect, e.g. *Elene*, 604-708. Mr. Smithson regards
the *Beowulf* as representing a stage of narrative development
somewhat more naïve than that attained by the four Christian
epics, which are characterized by single action, fewer digressions, more personal emotion, and swifter plot movement.[2] The
Christian epics center upon one person, but the *Beowulf* (like
the *Aeneid*) has to do not only with the hero but the effects
of his actions upon nations.

Smithson classifies the delays of plot movement thus: comments of the author on the action, episodes, digressions, repetitions. (He is discussing here only the *Juliana*, *Andreas*, and
Elene, setting aside the *Christ*, which is more lyrical than narrative.) The results of his comparison may be briefly summarized:

Of the first delay (comment by the author) *Juliana* affords
no example; *Elene* has six passages, 23 lines; *Andreas* contains four examples, 22 lines. The *Beowulf* has fifteen examples, 45 lines.

Of the second delay (episodes) *Juliana* and *Elene* furnish
no examples. There is one in the *Andreas*—a long one, however (555-817). The *Beowulf* contains three principal episodes: the scop's account of Sigemund (874-900), of Heremod
(910-15), of Finn and Hnaef (1068-1159),—133 lines in all.

Of the third delay (digressions) there are three examples
in *Juliana*, totalling 252 lines; one in *Elene*, 92 lines; three
in the *Andreas*, 122 lines. There are ten prominent digressions
in the *Beowulf*: the creation song (90-8); Hrothgar's account
of Beowulf's father (459-72); Unferth's taunt and Beowulf's
rejoinder (499-606); the story of the Brosing necklace (1197-

[2] *The Old English Christian Epic*, p. 398.

1214); Hrothgar's sermon to Beowulf (1709-84); contrast of Hygd and Thryth (1921-62); Beowulf's comment on the marriage of Freawaru and Ingeld (2024-69); Higelac's raid and the Swedish wars (2354-2400); the story of Hrethel and the battle of Ravenswood (2426-2509); the death of Higelac, fall of Haethcyn, wars of the Swedes and the Geats (2913-3007),—535 lines in all.

Of the fourth delay (repetition) there is but one example in *Juliana*, the two sections totalling 8 lines; two in the *Elene*, total 7 lines; no pure example in the *Andreas*, but two possible instances, making a total of 8 lines. Repetition is very common in the *Beowulf*. There are three separate accounts of the two chief episodes in the first part of the poem, —the fight with Grendel and the slaying of Grendel's mother. The first account of the fight with Grendel is given in lines 710-836, and the first account of the fight with his dam in lines 1251-1625. Beowulf later recounts these events to Hrothgar (957-79, 1651-70), and retells them to Higelac (1999-2147) upon his return home. There is much more variation in this latter report and more information is brought in which was not in the first versions of the two events. Nowhere in Beowulf's report to Higelac is there exact verbal repetition. There are other repetitions in the poem: Hrothgar's attitude of despair is mentioned three times (144-74, 929-42, 1769-81); Grendel's descent from Cain is related twice (102-14, 1263-6); Grendel's charmed life is mentioned twice (798-805, 987-90); the damage to Heorot is twice referred to (770-5, 997-1002). The contest with Grendel is summarized three times: 1267-76, 1333-7, 2349-54. Beowulf's victory over the fire-drake is referred to at least four times. The dragon is dead at line 2705. But his depredations and his final defeat are referred to in several places by the author, once in a summary (2826-45) and at other times

(2772, 2777-82, 2819-26). Then Wiglaf repeats the story of the victory of Beowulf and gives his last commands in lines 2873-83, 3084-100. The messenger goes over the same material in lines 2900-10. Repetition occurs again in the description of the dead monster in lines 3038-46. Aside from these repetitions, Higelac's death is referred to three times. It is difficult to estimate accurately the total of the lines of repetition in the *Beowulf;* Smithson puts the number at about 280. His summary of percentages is as follows:

	COMMENT	EPISODES	DIGRESSIONS	REPETITION
Juliana	0	0	33	0.6
Elene	1.7	0	6.9	1
Andreas	1.2	15.2	7	1
Beowulf	1.4	4.1	16.7	9

It might have been sufficient to give Smithson's conclusions upon his comparative study of the Old English epic, but his findings are for our present purpose exceedingly important in isolating the *Beowulf* from the other literature of its age, and some particulars of Mr. Smithson's investigations seemed to demand their place here. His opinion upon the large amount of repetition in the *Beowulf* he states thus: "The final poet of the *Beowulf*, I think, was familiar with the heroic epic, which was marked by repetition. . . . There is almost nothing in the Christian epics which we could not account for if we desired to do so, without going outside of the field of Old English literature." These epics were, he concludes "practically uninfluenced by the Vergilian epics." But the peculiarities of style which the *Beowulf* sustains in contrast to the plot-technique of the other epics of its age require us to look outside the field of Old English literature for a satisfactory comparison.

W. M. Hart (*Ballad and Epic*) shows that the *Beowulf* developed along lines quite unlike the growth of the vernacular ballads. The ballad-hero is seldom a sailor; but the sea, from the funeral-boat of Scyld to Beowulf's grave-mound, plays a large part in the English epic. The action of the poem is never far inland, and the sea is often, though somewhat vaguely, mentioned, e.g. in the description of Grendel's home. Beowulf's swimming match and the many kennings for "sea" and "ships" show a love for the ocean which is outside the range of the ballads. The king and his court come in for more attention in the *Beowulf* than is given to such elements in the ballads. Society in the epic rallies around the king. A defier of the king, an outlaw or an exile, is more often the typical ballad-hero. The power of the king is reflected in the splendor of his hall. The ballads never described a building equal to Heorot, the symbol of a great nation, gold-decorated, the center of social and religious feeling, symbolical of the very joys of living, the place where men eat and sleep. The lays do not develop the *comitatus* idea with anything like the completeness shown in the *Beowulf*. This must have come from a more pretentious model. The *Beowulf* is truly "national"; eighteen nations are named in it. This range is something which the lays cannot parallel. The *Beowulf* is concerned not only with the present but with the past and the future. The ballads never attempted to produce the effect of perspective which is gained in the epic by the frequent allusions to past events: the ravages of Grendel, the ancient hoard of the dragon, Beowulf's long reign, etc. With this must be added the tendency in the *Beowulf* to refer to family-lines. We can construct nearly complete genealogies from the bare text of the poem. There is nothing so precise as this in the ballads. Even Grendel is given a definite family connection. Sons' names are given in full with their patronymics: this is an established trait of the classic epic. No known gest or ballad contains a situation like the one described in the *Beowulf* in the hero's sponsorship of Heardred. It is hardly necessary to mention that abstract comment, reflection on death and the soul, generalizing, etc.—all elements beyond the range of the ballad —are prominent factors of the epic. Mr. Hart calls our attention to the fact that the poet had more ability in construction than we may be inclined to give him credit for: he could introduce digressions, then resume the thread of his story, making clear to the reader that he knew what he was about and not merely led out of his course by the attraction of a good story which he wanted to tack on to his epic for its own sake. This genius for construction he could not possibly have acquired from any body of ballad literature.[3]

Conflicts with History and Legendary Tradition

Beowulf is not an historic king. Contrary to rule, his name does not alliterate with those of the members of the family in which he is placed. He is as unsubstantial as the dragon; Chambers calls him "an intruder into the house of Hrethel."[4] Chambers furthermore can find no kernel of fact for the hero's part in Higelac's disaster; he raises the essential question, which has no answer in history: "Where was Beowulf, the protector of Heardred, when the young prince was slain by his enemies?" Other incongruous matters,—Beowulf's tottering throne at his death, just after he has concluded a glorious reign of fifty years; the improbability of Wiglaf's succes-

[3] Professor Lawrence summarizes his discussion of the extra-vernacular elements of the *Beowulf* thus: "Much descriptive and incidental matter was introduced, entirely foreign to the style of the *märchen*,—the sea voyage, the parley with the coast guard, the reception at Hrothgar's court, the banquets and present-giving, the long summary of the *Finnsburg* lay sung by Hrothgar's poet, the quarrel with Unferth, and the account of the swimming-exploit with Breca." *Beowulf and Epic Tradition*, p. 175.

J. E. Routh attempts to show that the irrelevant episodes and parentheses, so far from being evidence of the hand of an unskillful author, are common features of Anglo-Saxon poetic style. See his Study II in *Studies in the Ballad Theory of the Beowulf.*

[4] *Beowulf: An Introduction*, p. 10.

sion on the mere strength of his one exploit in the dragon-
fight; Beowulf's dying, an aged king, without making any
provisions for the future safety of his kingdom,—all combine
to make a picture which completely lacks historic foundation.[5]
The friendly relations between the Geats and the Danes, so
often referred to in the poem (without which, indeed, the
events in the first part of the poem cannot be imagined) "probably rest rather on fiction than on fact," to quote Professor
Lawrence.[6] The story of Beowulf's combats with monsters—
upon which his prowess as a doughty champion chiefly rests—
is without support in the Scandinavian folk-lore which is
supposed to furnish the basis for the main details of the
epic. True, the troll-fable appears in the *Grettis Saga*, but
without any antecedents in *Danish* hero-lore. Furthermore the
monster found in the Icelandic legends, the antagonist of
Bjarki (who has often been compared to Beowulf and perhaps
offers the closest analogy) cannot be said to be the counter-
part of Beowulf's winged dragon.[7] That Beowulf's dragon
may be allowed to claim an existence independent from any
other monster is Chambers' conclusion: "Indeed, of the in-
numerable dragon-stories extant, there is probably not one
which we can declare to be really identical with that of *Beowulf.*"[8] It is not now supposed that the *Beowulf* is a translation from a Scandinavian poem: it presents too many obvious dissimilarities to the body of Scandinavian literature as a
whole. It is founded on Scandinavian tradition, however,
probably acquired by the Angles before their migration from
the continent, and brought into England during the sixth
century. The cultural tone of the *Beowulf*, its meter and
style, differentiate it sharply from the old Norse sagas, and
indicate that they had little or nothing to do with giving the

---

[5] See further Lawrence, *Beowulf and Epic Tradition*, pp. 87, 96, 101, 105.
[6] *ibid.*, p. 47.   [7] See Chambers, *Beowulf, An Introduction*, p. 58.
[8] *ibid.*, p. 97.

poem its present shape.[9] Professor Lawrence finds in comparing the *Beowulf* and the *Edda* contrasts so violent as to preclude the possibility of any Scandinavian influence in the actual makeup of the Old English epic.[10]

The reader of the *Beowulf* feels that the author is striving for a point of view broader than one confined to the traditions of a single people. He chooses a Geat for his hero, and draws a picture of a great Danish dynasty. He is not overcome by the splendor of Hrothgar's court, however; the helplessness of the Danes before the depredations of Grendel is stressed in a way to show that the author was no slave to their traditions of grandeur. In the words of Mr. Chambers, "The poet's enthusiasm is not for the Danish race, as such, but for the ideal

---

[9] The form of the old Norse sagas is markedly different from the form of the *Beowulf*. The former are characterized by closed couplets, but the sequence of Anglo-Saxon verse generally allows the sense to be kept through an indefinite number of lines. Contrasted with the old Norse sagas as to content, the *Beowulf* shows characteristics still more at variance. Upon this head Wentworth Huyshe (*Beowulf, An Old English Epic*) says in the preface to his translation: "In the *Edda* we have tragedy in crude lumps, tangled masses of mystery without repose or symmetry. Scenes of dreadful violence, unredeemed by a single trait of human beauty or love, rush past us in a sort of picture-orgy. We see it all and feel it intensely, but the result is repulsion. The Hero-Saga of Iceland is all catastrophe; each lay is a roll of thunder, and it is over; with all its intense realism it is vague and momentary. It is different in *Beowulf*, for there we have a lay of 3,000 lines, within which the details are numerous, character is developed, difficulties overcome, a mode of life delineated, line by line the items of a three-fold situation (the three great deeds of Beowulf) accumulated with great art, a catastrophe not coming like a bursting rocket, but reined in, restrained, subtly approached, poetically handled."

[10] "There is nothing contrary to the evidence in the theory that a redactor of *Beowulf* may have had before him different versions of different parts of the poem, corresponding to one another, more or less, as *Atlamál* corresponds to the *Atlakviða*. This hypothesis, however, does not account for the difference in form between the English and the northern poems. No handling of the *Atlamál* or the *Atlakviða* could produce anything like the appearance of the *Beowulf*." Ker, *Epic and Romance*, p. 147.

See Chambers, *Beowulf, An Introduction* (347-52) for a refutation of the theory (chiefly supported by Stjerna) of the Scandinavian influence upon the poem.

of a great court with its body of retainers."[11] Mr. Lawrence
believes that the poet's description of Hrothgar's court sur-
passes anything in the experience of the author.[12] This is a
common epic trait. But our attention will be sharpened when
the poet departs radically from the social laws of the folk
among whom he lived and whose customs he was attempting
to mirror in his poem. Chambers[13] refers to Stjerna's dissatis-
faction with the poet's description of the cremation-rites. He
disagrees with the Scandinavian scholar's conclusions, drawn
from archaeological investigations, that the poet was combining
two accounts of Beowulf's funeral, in one of which the hero
was burnt, and in the other, buried; he does, however, admit
various discrepancies in the description and explains them as
due to the inaccurate knowledge which the Christian poet had
of the old heathen customs. Chambers does not agree with
Chadwick's contention that "the accuracy [of the funeral-
rites] is confirmed in every point by archaeological or contemporary literary evidence." He points to the burning of
the helmets and byrnies on Beowulf's pyre and, asking, "Were
the thegns asked to sacrifice theirs, and go naked into the next
fight in honour of their lord?" shows the absurdity of trying
to make this passage agree with what we know of Teutonic
burial-customs, and says that there is no archaeological con-
firmation for it. Thus the poet's description of one of the
most impressive events of his poem departs significantly from
local tradition. It will be shown later that his account closely
parallels similar passages in the *Aeneid*, which describe burial-
rites in considerable detail.[13a]

Archaeology furthermore cannot reconcile the profusion of
gold in the poem with the facts of Anglo-Saxon life as we

[11] *Beowulf, An Introduction*, p. 327.
[12] *Beowulf and Epic Tradition*, p. 49.
[13] *Beowulf, An Introduction*, p. 124.
[13a] See *post*, pp. 101 *ff*.

know them. This is one of Stjerna's arguments for the Scandinavian origin of the poem,—evidence which Clark Hall and Klaeber accept as proving that Norse customs had a great deal to do with giving the *Beowulf* its air of wealth and luxury. Chambers agrees that no gold-period comparable to that suggested in the *Beowulf* ever existed in Britain; but he refuses to accept this as evidence of Scandinavian coloring and inclines to let the poetic imagination of the author carry the responsibility of the exaggeration. Zappert apparently anticipates this statement: "Um einen hohen Begriff von der Schatzesherrlichkeit und Goldmacht ihrer Helden zu geben, bedienen sich unsere Epiker gewisser stehender Hyperbeln."[14] It is sufficient for our present purposes to hold fast to this point, namely, that the gold-adornments of the poem,—the decorations of Heorot, the armor and trappings of the warriors, the dragon's hoard, etc.—put the reader in mind of a gold-age which never existed among the Anglo-Saxons. This is another proof of the eclectic taste of the *Beowulf*-poet: he desired his poem to be *gold-fāh* and he gilded it according to his fancy, beyond the conditions and customs of the age in which he lived. Whether the gold in the *Beowulf* is Norwegian or Vergilian, it is not all English gold.

The *Beowulf* shows significant transgressions of the family- and tribal-codes which prevailed among the Teutonic people. The most remarkable instance of this nature is the flight of Beowulf's thegns during his dragon-fight. This is a monstrous thing, in defiance of the most fundamental principles of Anglo-Saxon loyalty. "The follower of a Teutonic king was expected to fight till death in defense of his lord."[15] Though the poet allows Wiglaf to upbraid the cowards most severely, he does not give us any explanation of their desertion. To say that they were merely cowards does not explain their defec-

---

[14] *Virgils Fortleben im Mittelalter*, p. 34.
[15] Chadwick, *The Origin of the English Nation*, p. 156.

tion, for they take to their heels near the beginning of the combat. If the poet had wanted to explain their desertion on these grounds, surely he would have had them show the white feather after Beowulf was wounded or when they themselves were attacked by the dragon. Apparently, they are not threatened. They had every call to prove their valor and stand by their lord; he had selected them especially for this deed of courage; he had been a wise and generous king to them—they had received many gifts from him, he had protected them from foreign oppression; he was now fighting not for his own glory but for the protection of their homes as much as for his own. And yet they deserted him; his picked warriors, equipped in armor which was the gift of their king, wearing the decorations which had been the pledge of fealty in the mead-hall, "his hand-companions stood not around him in war-valor." Classical tradition would have allowed a warrior to fight and run away; not so the tradition of the Teutonic folk. This act of desertion, not explained by the poet, must be kept in mind as a very outstanding case of anti-traditional plot-motivation in the poem. An attempt will be made later to explain it as an imitation of a prominent Vergilian motif.[15a]

A similar break with the warrior-code is to be found in the story of Hengest and Finn. Following the death of Hnaef, Hengest and his companions-in-arms come to terms with the slayer of their lord. Their code demanded that they die with Hnaef. Chadwick, commenting upon this breach of fealty, says that the defeated warriors made peace with Finn "for some unexplained reason." The *Beowulf*-poet doubtless took the story as he found it and did not attempt to justify the followers of Hnaef; the fact that he used this incident shows once again that he was not repugnant to including in his poem elements which did not consist with the tribal standards of the times of which he was writing. He must have known what

[15a] See *post*, pp. 119 *ff.*

a warrior's code demanded of him. According to the *Chronicle*, when Cyneheard slew Cynewulf all the followers of the slain leader refused the victor's terms (which were practically identical with those offered by Finn to the followers of Hnaef) and died as their leader had died—all but one, a British hostage, who was badly wounded. The same scene was repeated when Earl Osric attacked Cyneheard with a superior force: of Cyneheard's entire army only his godson survived, and he was wounded. The *Hrólfs Saga* relates that all of Hrólf's retinue perished with their king (cap. 52). Saxo writes that one man survived to play the part of the avenger.[16]

Another infraction of the warrior's code of honor is to be seen in the Onela-Eanmund story. Eanmund, the nephew of Onela, was slain by Weohstan, a follower of Onela. Chadwick remarks on this incident, that, "There can be no doubt that he [Onela] ought to have taken vengeance upon his knight [Weohstan]."[17] The poet's comment on the affair (*nō ymbe ðā fǣhðe sprǣc, / þēah ðe hē his brōðor bearn ābredwade*, 2618-19) indicates that he felt that Onela was not living up to his code in allowing his nephew's death to go unavenged; and affords another proof that the poet knew he was including anti-traditional material in the poem.

Peculiarities in Style: Latinisms

Aside from these broader inconsistencies which the *Beowulf* sustains with respect to Teutonic traditions, it exhibits a number of stylistic features which indicate traces of Latin influence. These Latinisms (which occur in the *Beowulf* in greater proportions than in other Anglo-Saxon poetry) in some instances seem to be definite Vergilian echoes; in any case they do not belong to the vernacular style. In examining these devices, refer-

---

[16] Chadwick, *Origin of the English Nation*, pp. 155-6.
[17] *Heroic Age*, p. 347.

ence will quite often be made to the *Aeneid*, not always with the intention of suggesting that the Vergilian passage is to be taken as the model of the passage quoted from the *Beowulf*, but merely to illustrate a characteristic form of the Latinism under consideration. Where there appears to be a striking similarity in word or phrase, attention will be invited to the possibility that there may be a real causal relation between the passages cited.

Chambers[18] shows that on the basis of Lichtenheld's test, the tendency in the *Beowulf* to drop the definite article before the combination *weak adjective + noun* shows a marked differentiation from the style of Cynewulf (who has been repeatedly upheld as having a share in the epic). Chambers' table (including the *Exodus*, which furnishes the nearest approach to the proportions of the *Beowulf*) shows the following frequency of the use of the definite article in phrases containing a *weak adjective + a noun*:

	WITH ARTICLE	WITHOUT ARTICLE
Juliana	27	3
Christ (II)	28	3
Elene	66	9
Guthlac (A)	42	6
Exodus	10	14
Beowulf	13	65

Commenting on these results, Chambers says, "The difference between *Beowulf* and the works of Cynewulf is too striking to be overlooked. In *Beowulf*, to every five examples without the article (e.g. *heaðostēapa helm*) we have *one* with the article (e.g. *se hearda helm*): in Cynewulf, to every five examples without the article we have *forty* with it."[19] This evidence forms an interesting note to Arnold's statement[20] that "the strength, the dignity, the deliberate march and conscious power which characterize the Epos were never within

[18] *Beowulf, An Introduction*, pp. 105-7.
[19] *ibid.*, p. 107.   [20] *Notes on Beowulf*, p. 120.

the reach of Cynewulf." In the light of this contrast between the *Beowulf* and the five other Old English poems, the absence of the definite article in Latin at once suggests itself as an explanation for this peculiarity of the Anglo-Saxon epic.

Passives. The use of the passive voice in the *Beowulf* where the active would seem to be more appropriate has been mentioned as a possible proof of Latin influence. Instances in the *Beowulf* are numerous: *wæs... helm ond byrne / ālȳsed* (1629-30); *wæs... gereorded* (1787-8); *wæs... þrȳðword sprecen* (642-3); *sceall gār wesan... hæfen* (3021-3); *wæs... hors gebǣted* (1399); *wæs... naca/ hladen* (1896-7); *bīoð ābrocene... āðsweord* (2063-4); *Ðā wæs hāten... Heort... gefrætwod* (991-2);[21] *wæs ful boren* (1192); *wæs... heardecg togen* (1288); *wæs... Bēowulf fetod* (1310); *Lāstas wǣron/... wīde gesȳne* (1402-3); *wæs heal roden* (1151); *wæs hord rāsod* (2283); *Wæs... wīg wīde gesȳne* (2316); *wæs ǣht boden* (2957). Commenting on this peculiarity, Klaeber says, "Ich habe den Eindruck, dass diese Eigentümlichkeit im Beowulf stärker hervortritt als in anderen ae. Gedichten."[22] There is a marked tendency in Vergil for the use of passives to call attention to the object of the action, rather than to the action itself: *caeduntur vigiles* (II, 266); *clarior ignis auditur* (II, 705); *Troia per undosum peteretur classibus aequor* (IV, 313); *vides toto properari litore* (IV, 416); *iuvenis... stridente sagitta... sternitur* (VII, 531-3); *Frangimur... fatis... ferimurque procella* (VII, 594); *Sternitur infelix Acron* (X, 730),[23] etc. Vergil's frequent omission of the auxiliary in the perfect form may be paralleled in the *Beowulf* by the not unusual omission of *wesan* (617, 1783, 1857, 2091, 2256, 2363, 2497, 2659); of *is* (2262, 3062);

---

[21] See Klaeber, Edition of *Beowulf*, Notes, p. 163.
[22] *Archiv*, 126, p. 355.
[23] See also I, 440, 574, 637-8, 700; II, 196; IV, 275-6, 466-7; VI, 45, 179; VII, 10; VIII, 262; X, 303-5, 622-3, etc.

of *syndon* (2035); and of *wæs* (811, 2297). The almost
formulary use of the passive forms of *gifan* and of *gifeðe* with
the auxiliary deserves special attention: *wæs . . . herespēd
gyfen* (64); *wæs . . . hilt . . . gyfen* (1677-8); *wearð / gyfen*
(1947-8); *gyfeþe wearð* (555); *gifeðe ne wæs* (2682);
gifeðe wæs (2491); *gifeðe . . . yrfeweard . . . wurde* (2730-
1); *gifeþe bið* (299); *wearð / gūðhrēð gyfeþe* (818-19).
Compare *non datur* (I, 409; VI, 140); *nec . . . datur* (VI,
327; *non dabitur* (VII, 313); *datur* (I,553; VI, 688; VII,
359; XI, 293); *dabitur* (IX, 116); *detur* (III, 7); *fortuna
dabatur* (II, 656); *spes dabatur* (II, 803); *sat datum* (II,
291; IX, 135); *dabitur . . . quod optas* (VII, 260), etc.

Superlatives in Relative Clauses. This feature is found in
the *Beowulf* in the following passages: *þāra þe hē cēnoste /
findan mihte* (206-7); *swylce hē þrýðlīcost / . . . findan
meahte* (2869-70); *swā hyt weorðlīcost / foresnotre men findan mihton* (3161-2). It is a common Latinism, found frequently in the *Aeneid: qui plurimus urbi / imminet* (I, 419-
20); *quae maxima. . . / . . Sol aspiciebat* (VII, 217-18); *quae
plurima vento / corripuit tabulas* (IX, 536-7); *quae plurima
. . . / enumerare vales* (IV, 333-4); *quae plurima caelo /
deicit* (VIII, 427-8); *natorum . . . fuerat qui maximus* (VII,
532); *ditissimus . . . / quae mittit dona* (IX, 360-1); *quarum
quae fandi doctissima* (X, 225); *qui maximus . . . / Aenean
petit* (X, 312-13); *ditissimus agri / qui fuit Ausonidum* (X,
563-4); *potuit quae plurima virtus / esse* (XI, 312-13); *quae
plurima mitti / . . . iubes* (XI, 352-3), etc.

Litotes. The marked preference exhibited by both epics
for this figure is one of the most important rhetorical features which they have in common. A single word is often
employed in the *Beowulf* to produce the effect of emphasis by understatement. Such are the uses of *undyrne* (127,
2911, 2000, 150, 410), *unlȳtel* (885, 498, 833), *unblīðe*
(130, 2268, 3031), *unmurnlīce* (449, 1756), *unforht* (287),

unforhte (444), *unsōfte* (1655, 2140), *unwāclīc* (3138),
etc. There are many more elaborate constructions: *Næs
ðā lang tō ðon* (2846, 2591), *næs ðǣr māra fyrst* (2555),
ne wæs hit lenge þā gēn (83), *Næs hit lengra fyrst* (134),
Nē þæt se āglǣca yldan þōhte (739)—cf. *Haud mora*
(III, 548; V, 749; VII, 156), *Haud fit mora* (X, 153),
nulla mora in Turno (XII, 11), *Aeneas Rutulum Sucronem
. . . haud multa morantem / excipit in latus* (XII, 505-7),
haud multa moratus (III, 610), *Nec Turnum segnis retinet
mora* (X, 308)—; *hē ne forwyrnde woroldrǣdenne* (1142),
ðū mē ne forwyrne (429)—cf. *nec . . . ire recuso* (II, 704),
Frangere nec . . . puppim . . . recuso (X, 297), *nec iussa recu-
sat Acestes* (V, 749), *nec quae pepigere recusent* (XII, 12),
neu praeceptis parere recusa (II, 607), *nec candida cursus /
luna negat* (VII, 8-9), *neque me Argolica de gente negabo* (II,
78); *non hoc mihi namque negares, / Omnipotens* (X, 614-
15)—; *nē mē swōr fela / āða on unriht* (2738-9)—cf. *nec
multum discrepat aetas* (X, 434)—; *lӯt manna ðāh / . . . þæt
hē wið attorsceaðan oreðe gerǣsde* (2836-39)—cf. *nec misero
clipei mora profuit aerei* (XII, 541)—; *Lӯt swīgode* (2897),
lӯt ǣnig mearn / þæt hī ofostlīce ūt geferedon / dӯre māðmas
(3129-31), *Nō þæt ӯðe byð* (1002)—cf. *nec visu facilis*
(III, 621)—; *næs ic him . . . lāðra ōwihte / . . . þonne his
bearna hwylc* (2432-3), *næs hīo hnāh . . . / nē tō gnēað gifa*
(1929-30), *Nē hūru Hildeburh herian þorfte / Ēotena trē-
owe* (1071-2), *Nealles Hetware hrēmge þorfton / fēðewīges*
(2363-4), *wæs gehwæþer ōðrum / lifigende lāð* (814-15),
ǣghwæðrum wæs / bealohycgendra brōga fram ōðrum
(2564-5),[24] *Nō his līfgedāl / sārlīc þūhte secga ǣnegum*
(841-2), *nē his līfdagas . . . . / nytte tealde* (793-4), (These
two passages last quoted refer to the death of Grendel.)
nealles druncne slōg / heorðgenēatas (2179-80), *Ðone sīðfæt*

---

[24] In reference to these last two citations, see Klaeber's edition of *Beowulf*,
Notes, p. 153.

him snotere ceorlas / lȳthwōn lōgon . . . . / hwetton higerōfne (202-4), *ne bið swylc earges sīð* (2541), *feorhsweng ne oftēah* (2489), *hond sweng ne oftēah* (1520). The following examples from the *Aeneid* may also be adduced for comparison's sake: *Venus haud animo nequiquam exterrita mater* (VIII, 370); *magnorum haud umquam indignus avorum* (XII, 649); *nec me meminisse pigebit Elissae* (IV, 335); *Sunt aliae innuptae . . . / nec genus indecores* (XII, 24-5).

Anaphora, Polysyndeton. These pleonastic constructions are to be found in the *Beowulf* in the following passages: *Anaphora—hwīlum . . . hwīlum . . . hwīlum . . . hwīlum* (2107-11); *hwīlum . . . hwīlum* (2016-20). *Polysyndeton—gē . . . gē* (1864, 1248); *oððe . . . oððe . . . oððe . . . oððe . . . oððe . . . oððe . . . oððe* (1763-6); *nō . . . nē . . . nē . . . nē* (1392-4, 1735-7); *ne . . . nē* (2628); *ne . . . nē* (2738). The rhetorical effect of these passages is very strongly suggestive of Latin influence.[25] These figures are favorites with Vergil, and may be found on nearly every page of the *Aeneid*. Following is a list which may be indefinitely extended: *aut . . . aut* (I, 396, 183, 361-2, 527-8; II, 36-8; IV, 186-7; V, 448-9; VI, 365-7, 454; VII, 164, 307, 721; VIII, 317, 613-14; IX, 186, 608, 686-7; X, 9-10, 135, 449-50, 806); *nunc . . . nunc* (I, 220-1; IV, 74-7, 285, 442; V, 441, 457, 701; VI, 315; VIII, 20; X, 355, 368, 680; XI, 86, 625-7, 650-1; XII, 476); *nunc . . . nunc . . . nunc* (I, 751-2; IV, 376-7; V, 156-7, 586-7); *simul . . . simul* (I, 631-2; II, 220-2; IX, 318-19); *hic . . . hic* (I, 427; III, 399-401; VIII, 724-5; XII, 479); *hic . . . hic . . . hic . . . hic* (II, 29-30); *hanc . . . hanc* (VIII, 357); *hos . . . hos* (XI, 766); *hinc . . . hinc* (X, 433-4; IV, 40-2; VIII, 473-4; X, 760; XII, 745); *pars . . . pars* (VII, 686-7; XI, 888-9; XII, 278; I, 423-5; IV, 405-6; VI, 6-7, 491-2, 642-4); *pars . . . pars . . . pars* (VII, 624-6); *miratur*

[25] See *Archiv* 126, pp. 358-9.

. . . *miratur* (I, 421-2); *mirantur* . . . *mirantur* (I, 709); *hoc primum* . . . *hic primum* (I, 450-1); *sternit* . . . *sternit* (II, 306); *ubique* . . . *ubique* (II, 368-9); *vidi* . . . *vidi* (II, 499-501); *ter* . . . *ter* (II, 792-3; VI, 700-1).

The Use of the Gerund. The Gerund, or dative infinitive, used in the *Beowulf* furnishes a parallel to Latin gerundive forms. The preference of the author for this construction may be seen from the following list: *tō gegangenne* (2416); *tō befleônne* (1003); *tō farenne* (1805); *tō healdanne* (1731); *tō gesēcanne* (1922); *tō efnanne* (1941); *tō reccenne* (2093); *tō gebīdanne* (2445, 2453); *tō sēceanne* (2562); *tō gecēosenne* (1851); *tō gefremmanne* (174, 2644); *tō gecȳðanne* (257); *tō geþolianne* (1419).

Periphrastic Forms. These have been discussed as proofs of Latin influence.[26] These constructions are to be found in the following passages of the *Beowulf: se æglǣca ēhtende wæs* (159); *ðæs morþorhetes myndgiend wǣre* (1105); *se secg hwata secggende wæs / lāðra spella* (3028-9).

The Appositive Participle. The frequent use of the appositive participle in the *Beowulf* may be taken as another evidence of the Latinity of the poem. There exist ninety-one instances of the use of this construction: 23 in the present, 68 in the past form; there are 6 others (1945, 304, 1031, 2229, 2230, 3151) of which classification is impossible, usually because of imperfections of the text. The present participle is used without an object 19 times: lines 2272, 2569, 815, 2219, 2235, 2548, 708, 2062, 2716, 1953, 916, 535, 1389, 2850, 1187, 2781, 372, 46, 1581. It occurs with an object 4 times: lines 2106, 2350, 1227, 1829. The past participle occurs without an object 18 times: lines 1351, 2569, 846, 1370, 2852, 868, 262, 1913, 2443, 614, 1948, 3012, 3085, 1819, 59, 3049,

---

[26] See C. Pessels, *The Present and Past Periphrastic Tenses in Anglo-Saxon,* Johns Hopkins Press, 1896, pp. 49 ff., 81 ff.

1479, 1937. There are 50 examples with an object: lines 1113, 721, 1275, 1451, 2274, 2595, 531, 1467, 2580, 3117, 2359, 2401, 2111, 923, 217, 630, 2309, 1005, 975, 1368, 1285, 250, 1450, 1038, 1645, 2255, 845, 1443, 3018, 1333, 777, 624, 553, 406, 2680, 2764, 2441, 3146, 1126, 480, 3014, 3139, 2931, 2192, 1900, 1531, 2769, 1028, 2762, 871. This construction therefore occurs in the *Beowulf* about once in every 33 lines. Its common use in the poem and elsewhere in Anglo-Saxon induces Morgan Callaway to believe that "the appositive use of the present and past participle in Anglo-Saxon is due to Latin influence."[27] He quotes Einenkel *Mittelenglische Syntax* (Münster 1887), p. 273, to substantiate his opinion. Referring to the adverbial use of the participle to denote manner, he says that, although this use is more common in the *Beowulf* than elsewhere, it cannot be regarded as due to specific Latin influence, which would be expected to appear in Old English writings for which there is a Latin original, but is rather a proof of the early taking-over of the Latin construction into the whole body of the vernacular.

Hātan *Followed by the Infinitive.* This is the usual construction with *hātan;* the only exception occurs in the use of the *þæt* clause, lines 2156-7: *hēt / þæt ic his ǣrest ðē ēst gesægde.* The Latin usage is identical here: in only three cases does Vergil use *iubeo* without the infinitive: VII, 432; IX, 117; X, 53. The construction occurs in the *Beowulf* 21 times: lines 1035-6, 1053-4, 1808, 2337, 2892, 198-9, 391, 1114-15, 1920-1, 2152, 2190, 3095, 3110, 293-6, 386, 2802, 674, 1868-9, 1045, 2812, 991. This last construction represents a passive use of the verb: *Đā wæs hāten . . . Heort . . . /ˀ . . . gefrætwod,* which may be paralleled in the *Aeneid: indicere bella Latinus / . . . iubebatur tristesque recludere portas* (VII, 616-17); *ad hunc alii cursum contendere iussi* (V, 834). The

[27] See *Publications of the Modern Language Association,* 16, p. 297.

other passages containing *iubeo* followed by an infinitive phrase number 51 in the *Aeneid*: II, 3; III, 289, 88; V, 849; XI, 353; I, 648; II, 146; III, 267; IV, 270; V, 15, 552, 757, 773, 828; VII, 154, 276, 468; VIII, 175; X, 858; XI, 79, 83, 240; XII, 111; II, 37; III, 261; VI, 632; VIII, 498; X, 179; XI, 218; XII, 584; III, 9, 472; VIII, 646; V, 386; I, 577; IV, 546; IX, 101; XII, 189; II, 186; III, 162; V, 359; VII, 428; IX, 233; XII, 854; IV, 346; X, 222; XII, 824; III, 101, 146; V, 385; X, 242.

Repetition of Stock Phrases. Both poems show a tendency to use conventional phrases to express meanings like "the saying is," "as I have heard," etc. *Mīne gefrǣge* is a favorite with the *Beowulf*-poet; he employs it 5 times: lines 776, 837, 1955, 2685, 2837,—*gefrǣge* not being used outside this combination, which is found only in poetry. *Hȳrde ic* is employed 4 times: lines 38, 62, 2163, 2172. Comparable to these phrases are certain conventional expressions, carrying the same meaning, used frequently in the *Aeneid*: *Fama volat* (III, 121; VIII, 554; VII, 392); *fama . . . advolat* (X, 510-11); *Fama volans . . . moenia replet* (XI, 139-40); *volitans . . . Fama . . . tulerat* (VII, 104-5); *Fama . . . detulit* (IV, 298-9); *Fama ruit* (IX, 474); *it Fama* (IV, 173); *fama est* (III, 578, 694; VI, 14; VIII, 600; X, 641; XII, 735).

The introduction *fēa worda cwæð* is twice used in the *Beowulf*: lines 2662, 2246. Similar introductory phrases occur often in the *Aeneid*: *sic pauca refert* (VIII, 154); *Tandem pauca refert* (IV, 333); *pauca refert* (X, 17); *paucis affatur* (XII, 71); *paucis docebo* (XI, 315); *Paucis ita reddidit* (VI, 672); *breviter sic fatur* (X, 621); *breviter fata est* (VI, 398, 321); *breviter affata . . . est* (VI, 538); *tum breviter . . . affata* (IV, 632); *breviter . . . ait* (IX, 353-5); *tum breviter . . . profatur* (I, 561); *tum breviter . . . precatur* (X, 251).

It is in accord with classic precedent to give the father's

name with the name of the son. Introducing the hero's speeches, Beowulf's ancestry is thus referred to 9 times, (with *maþelode*); lines 529, 631, 957, 1383, 1473, 1651, 1817, 1999, (*maþelade*) 2425. Similarly, at the beginning of Unferth's speech, he is called *Ecglāfes bearn* (499), and Wiglaf is twice referred to as *Wēohstānes sunu* (2862, 3076). The 39 uses of the word *sunu* illustrate 28 cases of an accompanying proper noun in the genitive case. *Bearn* is used 40 times: in 16 cases it is accompanied by a proper noun in the genitive case. The expression *Gēata bearn* (2184) is paralleled by a variety of compounds in the *Aeneid*: *Troiugena* (III, 359; VIII, 117; XII, 626); *Iliades* (used 6 times); *Dardanides* (used 22 times); *Anchisiades* (used 6 times), etc. The hero of the *Aeneid* is poetically referred to as the son of Anchises 5 times; lines V, 244, 424; VI, 322, 331; VII, 152.[28]

Latin Loan-Words. The list of words of classical origin which are to be found in the *Beowulf*, though not extensive, forms an important element of the vocabulary of the poem:

Draca (892, 2211, 2088, 2290, 2549, 2402, 3131. Compounds: *eorðdraca* 2712, 2825; *fȳrdraca* 2689; *līgdraca* 2333, 3040; *nīðdraca* 2273; *sǣdraca* 1426). This word is a loanword adapted from *draco*.[29] The 13 uses of the word in its simple form or in compounds would indicate that the author regarded it as an equivalent of the word *wyrm*, the standard

---

[28] With the verb *maþelian* the following formula occurs 3 times: *Hrōðgār maþelode, helm Scyldinga*, 371, 456, 1321. *Swā hit gedēfe wæs* (*bið*) is used 3 times: 561, 1670, 3174. *On þǣm dæge þysses līfes* occurs in the following lines: 197, 790, 806. *Þæt wæs gōd cyning* is found in lines 11, 863, 2390. This expression occurs in the latter half of the line; in line 11 it seems to be exclamatory, and in the other two cases, especially in line 2390, it appears to be used merely as a convenient ending to a verse-paragraph. The hendiadys "feud and crime" occurs 4 times;; *fǣhðe ond fyrene* (137, 2480), *fǣhðe ond fyrena* (879), *fyrene ond fǣhðe* (153). *Heard under helme* occurs in lines 404, 342, 2539; *hyne fyrwet bræc* in lines 1985, 2784, 232—*hine fyrwyt; secg on searwum* in lines 249, 2700, 2530—*secgas.*

[29] Skeat, *Etymological Dictionary; N.E.D.*

native word, which is employed 22 times. Four of the compounds (*eorðdraca*, *fȳrdraca*, *līgdraca*, and *nīðdraca*) are peculiar to the *Beowulf* alone.

Dēofol (2088, 756, 1680). This word derives from *diabolus*, passing through the forms *diabul*, *diavol*, *ia* changing through *io* to *éo*.[30] "The forms in the other Teutonic languages [the Gothic excepted] were partly at least from Latin and probably adopted more or less independently of each other."[31]

Candel (1572; *woruldcandel* 1965—found only in the *Beowulf*). The Latin original is *candela*.[32] "One of the Latin words introduced at the English Conversion, and long associated chiefly with religious observances. This sacred character of the word bears on the O.E. poetic compounds *Gōdes candel*, *heofoncandel*, etc."[33]

Symbel (81, 489, 1008, 564, 619, 1010, 2431, 1232, 119, 2104; *symbelwyn* 1782). This word is an adaptation of the Latin *symbola*[34] which means a "contribution to a feast." It is used in Old English to mean "feast."

Gīgant (113, 1562, 1690). *Gigas* (accusative *gigantem*) is the word from which the Old English word is adapted.[35]

Gim (2072; *searogim* 1157, 3102, 2749). This word is adapted from *gemma*.[36] Compare the O.H.G. feminine form of the word: *gimma*.

Weall (229, 572, 1224, 2323, 785, 891, 1573, 2307, 2526, 2542, 2716, 2759, 3060, 3103, 3161, 326. Compounds *bordweall* 2980; *eorðweall* 2957, 3090; *sǣweall* 1924; *scildweall* 3118). This derives from *vallum*.[37]

Mīlgemearc (1362). Of *mīl-* Skeat says, "It is formed from the Latin plural *milia*, used in the sense of a Roman mile."

[30] Skeat, J. C. Hall, *Anglo-Saxon Dictionary*.
[31] *N.E.D.*   [32] Hall, Skeat, *N.E.D.*   [33] *N.E.D.*   [34] *N.E.D.*
[35] Hall, Skeat, *N.E.D.*   [36] Hall, Skeat, *N.E.D.*
[37] Hall, *N.E.D.*—"not a Teutonic word, but borrowed from the Latin *vallum*, a rampart."

Strǣt (320, 916, 1634. Compounds: *merestrǣt*, 514; *lagu-strǣt* 239—found only in the *Beowulf*). Skeat says the word derives "from *strata* for *strata via*."[38] Note *miratur . . . strata viarum* (*stratas vias*, I, 422).[39]

Ancor (303, 1883; *ancorbend* 1918—found in the *Beowulf* only). This is a loan-word from the original *ancora*.[40]

Wīn (1467, 1162, 1233; *wīnærn* 654). Derived from the Latin *vinum*.[41]

Cēap (2415, 2482). The late Latin *caupo* has been suggested as the original of this word,—"probably from *caupo*—huckster, innkeeper."[42] Upon this, the *N.E.D.* says "there are serious difficulties."[43]

Disc (3048, 2775). As "dish" adapted from *discus*.[44]

Camp (2505—emendation Klaeber, Chambers). Speaking of the use of this word to mean "battle," Skeat says, "Notwithstanding the widespread use of the word in this sense, it is certainly non-Teutonic, and borrowed from Latin *campus*, in late Latin 'a battle.' "[45] DuCange defines the word thus: "Duellum ipsum, quod in campo seu arena initur." *Campus* occurs 79 times in the *Aeneid;* quite frequently, especially in the last 5 books, Vergil uses it in the sense of "battle-field."

Or (1688, 1041, 2407). Klaeber's Glossary to his Edition of *Beowulf* suggests that this word is connected with the Latin *ora*. Further substantiation for this affinity seems to be lacking. *Ora* occurs 50 times in the *Aeneid*, usually in the sense of "shores."

Orcnêas (112—found in the *Beowulf* only). Skeat defines *orc* (*ork*) thus: "From Latin *orca*, a sea-fish, perhaps the narwhal." Of the same word, Weekley says, "Vaguely used, by

---

[38] cf. Hall, *N.E.D.*
[39] Lejay, edition of the *Aeneid*, note on the line.
[40] Hall, Skeat, *N.E.D.*   [41] Hall, Skeat, *N.E.D.*
[42] Weekley, *Etymological Dictionary of Modern English.*
[43] cf. DuCange, *Glossarium Mediae et Infimae Latinitatis.*
[44] Skeat, *N.E.D.*   [45] cf. Hall.

association, with Latin *Orcus*, hell of mythological monsters in general." The *N.E.D.* agrees with this shift of meaning.[46]

Orc (3047, 2760). Adaptation from *orca*, late Latin.[47]

Ceasterbūend (768—found only in the *Beowulf*). Of the first element of this compound, the *N.E.D.* (entry, *Chester*) says, "This is one of the best ascertained of the Latin words adopted by the Angles and Saxons during the conquest of Britain." The original word is *castra*.

Segn (1204, 2776, 2767, 47, 1021, 2958; *hēafodsegn* 2152). This word is carried over from *signum*.[48]

Cempa (1312, 1551, 1585, 2078, 1761, 1948, 2044, 2502, 2626, 206; *fēþecempa* 1544, 2853—found only in the *Beowulf*). This word probably derives from the late Latin *campio*, accusative *campionem*. "Kluge and others claim the word as native Teutonic, mainly on the ground of the improbability that the Germans, who had so many native words to designate war, should adopt a foreign designation; but they offer no satisfactory account of its etymology."[49] Skeat inclines to see in the word "champion" a derivation from *cempa* and *campionem*.

Nōn (1600). Derivative from *nona* (*-hora*).[50]

Wīc (125, 1125, 1612, 3083, 1304, 821, 2589; *wīcstede* 2462, 2607; *dēaþwīc* 1275; *hrēawīc* 1214—the latter two not found outside the *Beowulf*). "Not English but borrowed from Latin *vicus*."[51]

Cumbol (2505). The earlier form of this word (which is found only in poetry) is *cuml* or *cumol*, meaning "cairn," and derives from *cumulus*. A. S. Cook suggests[52] that "from meaning 'cairn,' the permanent sign of what is ever memorable," the word may have "come to mean 'sign' in general, and that by which the sign or signal is given."

[46] cf. *Anglia*, 36, p. 169.   [47] Hall. cf. Skeat, *N.E.D.*   [48] Hall, *N.E.D.*
[49] *N.E.D.*   [50] cf. Skeat, Hall.   [51] Skeat. cf. *N.E.D.*
[52] *Modern Language Notes*, III, 6.

Sigle (1200, 1157, 3163; *māððumsigle* 2757,—found only in the *Beowulf*). This word may have an affinity with the late Latin *sigillum* (plural *sigilla*), the diminutive of *signum*. A form nearly akin to it is *sigil*, meaning "seal" or "signet."[53]

Secg (208, 249, 402, 871, 980, 1311, 1569, 1812, 2226, 2352, 2406, 2700, 2708, 2863, 3028, 3071, 2019, 1379, 213, 2530, 3128, 633, 842, 947, 996, 1672, 1759, 2252, 490). This word, meaning "man," "warrior," may derive from *socius*. The Latin word is used (usually with the meaning "companion-in-arms") 104 times in the *Aeneid*.[54]

Secg (684). There is a possible affinity of this word (meaning "sword") to the Latin word *secare*. From *secg* derives the modern form "sedge"—a plant having hard sharp leaves. The *N.E.D.* suggests that the word is originally Indo-Germanic, *secare* containing the same root. The word *gladiolus* is referred to as illustrating a similar blending of meanings, i.e., sword-like plant leaves.

Wer (105, 1352, 1268, 3172, 216, 1222, 1233, 1440, 1650, 120, 993, 1731, 3000, 2947, 1256). According to the *N.E.D.*, this word is a regular phonetic descendant of *vir*.[55]

---

[53] *N.E.D.*

[54] See Klaeber's Glossary to his edition of *Beowulf*.

[55] cf. *Anglia*, XXXI, 261.

There are in the *Beowulf* many nouns in the accusative form which indicate extent of time and space. While it cannot be said that the poet felt the Latinity of these case-forms, nevertheless the frequent occurrence of them in the poem suggests an interesting comparison with the parallel usage in Latin. A partial list follows: *longe hwīle* (2780); *lange hwīle* (2159, 16); *lange þrāge* (114); *longe þrāge* (54); *lȳtel fæc* (2240); *seofon niht* (517); *lȳtle hwīle* (2097); *fōtes trem* (2525); *ondlonge niht* (2938); *morgenlongne dæg* (2894); *andlangne dæg* (2115); *āne hwīle* (1762); *ænige hwīle* (2548); *læssan hwīle* (2571); *hwīle* (2137).

Lastly it may be mentioned that the use of conventional plurals, especially of abstract nouns, suggests foreign influence (see *Archiv*, 126, p. 254). The following examples may be noted: *gryrum ecga* (483)—cf. *armorum horror* (11, 301); *heortan wylmas* (2507); *wintrys wylmum* (516); *cearwylmas* (282); *cearwælmum* (2066); *sorhwylmas* (904); *sorhwylmum* (1993); *hondrǣs hæleða* (2072); *wonsceaft wera* (120); *hordmāðum hæleþa* (1198), etc.

Chapter IV

Broad Similarities in the *Aeneid* and the *Beowulf*

THE two epics exhibit many similarities in social conditions, and contain many statements, direct and indirect, of the authors' opinions regarding human destiny and divine influence: all of which provide a background of a kind sufficiently harmonious that we are encouraged to examine certain specific features of the *Beowulf* where the resemblances seem to be most definite.

Family consciousness, for instance, is a deep-founded trait of both poems. One can hardly think of the hero of the *Aeneid* without remembering his departure from burning Troy, supporting his father upon his shoulders and clasping the hand of his son, whom the shade of his wife has just committed to his care. Other family groups stand forth prominently: Evander and Pallas, Euryalus and his mother, Turnus and his sister Juturna, Camilla and her father, the house of Priam, the house of Latinus, etc. Family units in the *Beowulf* are equally prominent: Hrothgar and his queen and sons, the house of Hrethel, the family of the Swedish king, Ongentheow, etc. Both Turnus and Beowulf at their deaths refer to their relations to their families: Beowulf rejoices to say that he is not guilty of kin-murder (2741-3), and the Latin hero determines to die worthy of his ancestors (XII, 648-9).

Transposition of Narrative Material. The reader feels that the action in neither epic depends upon suspense as an element of heightening interest in the story. Quite often the outcome of an episode is told at the beginning, and nothing is left to the imagination. For Vergil, oracular utterances, divine portents, and the visitation of gods operate to make clear the events of the climaxes of his poem; the *Beowulf*-poet does not have recourse to such roundabout devices, but tells us plainly at the outset what the conclusion of a particular incident is to be. Commenting upon this, Professor Lawrence says, "There was no objection to anticipating the outcome, since this was already known. Interest in heroic story lay, not in suspense, but in opportunities for emotional effect afforded by tragic complications and for alluring details of narrative."[1] The speech of Jove to Venus (I, 257-96) suggests the entire purpose of the *Aeneid*. Here the father of the gods, after hinting at the labors of Aeneas, shows the working-out of the *fatum Romanum*. He tells of the Latin wars, the birth of Romulus and Remus, and the dynasties of the Cæsars. Vergil evidently did not presume that his readers should require suspense as a whet to their interests. We are all the more interested in observing the ingenious means which he employed to render attractive a story whose conclusion had been disclosed. It is easy to multiply instances: the oracle of the Ortygian Apollo (III, 154-71) plainly outlines to Aeneas the course he is to follow to the Ausonian fields; when the Trojans first touch the coast of Italy they see four white horses in the plain, which omen Anchises reads as a sign of war (III, 537-40); Aeneas at the court of Carthage is warned by Mercury (IV, 265-76; 560-70) to make his escape from the wrath of the injured queen; the Sibyl (VI, 83-97) and Anchises (VI, 756-853) foretell to Aeneas the outcome of the *fatum Romanum*. Over and over again this certainty of success recurs to him in the midst of the doubtful battles on the fields of Latium. (See XI, 112-13; XII, 187-90; also VII, 239-40; VIII, 131-3; XI, 305-7.) How deeply Vergil wished to im-

[1] *Beowulf and Epic Tradition*, p. 113.

press upon the mind of the reader the fact of the coming power
of Rome is seen once again in the description of the shield of
Aeneas (VIII, 626-731), where the event of the whole poem
is once more set forth. The outcome of the combat with Turnus
is a foregone conclusion; but the very absence of suspense as to
the event of the struggle adds to the dire solemnity of the scene
with which the *Aeneid* closes. Turning to the Old English epic,
we see that Beowulf's death is plainly foretold to the reader, as
it is also clearly foreshadowed to the hero himself. (See 2419-
24, 2586-91.) No less unmistakable were these warnings to the
aged king than was the bird of ill omen to the doomed Turnus. This penchant of the *Beowulf*-poet for hinting at future
tragedy is to be seen in his frequent ominous references to the
later destiny of Heorot. The first mention of the completed
building must include a mention of its fate (81-3), which is
connected with a larger disaster (83-5). In lines 781-2 the
burning of Heorot is again foretold. Beowulf's long report
to his liege-lord Higelac contains a prophecy of war between
the Danes and the Heathobards (2029-69). The poet was
so possessed with the turn of foretelling events to come, that
in this latter case ordinary probability is completely sacrificed. It would have been sufficient to allow Beowulf to express his opinion that no good would come of the alliance of
Ingeld and Freawaru; but to allow him to be so good an oracle
is exceeding the bounds of reason. The *Beowulf*-poet needed
his *vates;* without the divine aids of which Vergil made such
free use, he was obliged to risk exceeding human powers and
occasionally have his men speak like gods.[2] Again, Hrothgar's
remark about the purpose of Beowulf's coming is something
of a divination (lines 381 *ff.*). The Danish king is represented as giving thanks to God for a deliverance to be accom-
plished by a hero whom he has not seen, whose purposes

[2] See Lawrence, *Beowulf and Epic Tradition*, p. 80.

he does not know. Hrothgar's premonition is suggestively
like Evander's devout reminiscence (VIII, 200 *ff.*). The situa-
ations are identical here: a pious king speaks of deliverance
from a scourge to be wrought by a foreign champion. Furthermore, the messenger of Beowulf's death states his forebodings of the misfortunes to come upon the Geats from the
Swedes after the death of the hero (2999-3027). The same
tendency appears in a happier tone in Hrothgar's remark to
Beowulf, prophesying future success to the young hero as a
ruler of the Sea-Geats (1845-53). The fate of Hondscio is
plainly mentioned as foredoomed (2076-7); so is the fate of
Aeschere (1240-1, 1251-2). Grendel's defeat is as clearly
foretold (734-6).

Both epics, as the foregoing instances show, give proof of a
tendency to look ahead to events which occur in the action
posterior to the time of the mention of the events. This taste
for the transposition of references is to be seen many times
elsewhere in the *Beowulf;* quite often we are told of events
in the past which link with the present action of the narrative.
The past history of the treasure guarded by the fire-drake is
related partially in several passages: in lines 2231-71, for
instance, which relate how a last survivor of an illustrious
race hid the hoard in the earth; and in lines 3047-75 (an older
version of the tale), where it is stated that the treasure was
buried by famous warriors who laid a curse upon it.[3] It may
be mentioned here that the *Aeneid* contains similar passages
which refer to the past history of treasure-hoards: I, 358-9;
X, 526-8. Klaeber remarks that the turn of the moral expressed in lines 2764-6 is "an apparently uncalled for ethical
reflection on the pernicious influence of gold."[4] Comments of
this kind are frequent in the *Aeneid*: one recalls (I, 349-51)

---

[3] Lawrence, *Beowulf and Epic Tradition*, pp. 213-21.

[4] Notes, Edition of *Beowulf*, p. 209. These are the lines in question: *Sinc
ēaðe mæg, / gold on grunde gumcynnes gehwone / oferhīgian, hȳde sē ðe wylle!*

the slaying of Sychaeus by Pygmalion (*auri caecus amore*) ; the betrayal of Polydore (III, 55-7) and Vergil's reflection, *Quid non mortalia pectora cogis, / auri sacra fames!* (Cf. also VIII, 327.)[5]

Comments and partly sketched details referring to the past life of the hero are brought (sometimes rather awkwardly) into the narrative of the *Beowulf*. These appear in his own reminiscences of his youth (2428-34) before attacking the dragon and in his review of his life as a king (2732-9). The author goes back to the period of his hero's immaturity (2183-9) and presents him in the light of the typical folk-tale hero, a youth of small promise. Beowulf's part in Higelac's last battle is referred to in lines 2359-79, and 2501-8. Further scattered references to Higelac's unlucky raid are to be found in lines 1202-9, 2354-9, and 2913-20. Vergil shows a like taste for relating in greater or less detail the histories of various characters of his poem; however much Beowulf's reminiscences during his dragon-fight seem to be out of place, they are not more incongruous to the action than is Vergil's lengthy review of the history of the youth of Camilla (XI, 535-94), recounted by Diana, in the midst of the description of cavalry charges and ambuscades. Books Two and Three of the *Aeneid*, which review in the hero's own words his adventures up to the time in which he is relating them, have a parallel in Beowulf's account of his exploits before his appearance at the court of Hrothgar (419-24, combats with giants and nickers; 535-81, swimming-victory over Breca). Some of the characters in Hades are allowed to relate personal histories of considerable length: e.g. Palinurus' story (VI, 347-71), and the tale

---

[5] There is also a strong Christian foundation for this sentiment in the *Beowulf*. Zappert comments thus on the reference: "Denn wie im Leben legt auch im Epos Mammon sein Schwergewicht in die Schale der Entscheidung, und vergebens stossen heidnische wie christliche Dichter bei solchen Anlässen ihre moralischen Seufzer aus." *Virgils Fortleben im Mittelalter*, p. 8.

of Deiphobus (VI, 509-34). The Sibyl tells Aeneas the tale of Salmoneus (VI, 585-94). The story of future Rome, portrayed on the shield of Aeneas (VIII, 626-731), is the sequel to the story of the fall of Troy, wrought in the entablature of Dido's temple (I, 453-93). The harking-back to previous instances in the *Beowulf* is to be noted also in the references of Grendel's previous depredations, of which mention is made somewhat unnecessarily in the course of the narrative: lines 716-17, 1579-84.

The many references in the *Beowulf* to events loosely connected with the action, or entirely separate from it, produce to the mind of the modern reader the effect of unartistic digression. But it may be assumed that the annoying half-hints of the tragedy of Finn, for instance, the treachery of Heremod, the story of Thryth, the tale of the Brosing necklace, the battle at Ravenswood, the burning of Heorot, and many other dimly sketched happenings, were fully known to the audience who had heard the old lays and who heard the poem itself recited or read. Thus the poet (with an economy, however, which at times seems to fit ill with his lavish repetition) might employ a mere name which he knew was sufficient to bring to the minds of his audience the whole background of a tale as complex perhaps as the story of the fall of the house of Priam.[6]

The Heroic Element. Although the outcome of a crisis in the *Beowulf* is usually foretold, the poet may heighten interest in it by allowing the combatants to be so evenly matched that the reader may be sure of a good fight. Breca was no mean

[6] See Lawrence, *Beowulf and Epic Tradition*, p. 22. An instance of this kind may be found in the *Aeneid*, though the episodes in that poem are usually given in more satisfactory detail. It is said that, in explanation of the portent of Acestes' arrow taking fire in the air, the soothsayers foretold the happenings which it presaged: *Docuit post exitus ingens / seraque terrifici cecinerunt omina vates* (V, 523-4). We are not told what the omens represented, but the issue probably was understood by Vergil's hearers.

antagonist for the victorious hero, and Beowulf succumbed to
the dragon only after a brave resistance. The most dramatic
situation of this kind occurs in the hero's encounter with
Grendel's dam. As one sees the Geat struggling in the clutch
of the monster, he feels a sympathetic tenseness not unlike the
emotions aroused by Vergil's description of Priam's death at
the hands of Pyrrhus, or Turnus lying helpless beneath the
spear of Aeneas. The poet emphasizes Beowulf's danger:
*Hæfde ðā forsīðod sunu Ecgþēowes / under gynne grund . . .
/ nemne him heaðobyrne helpe gefremede / . . . ond hālig
God / gewēold wīgsigor* (1550-4). Beowulf recalls his hard
straits in his report to Hrothgar: *Ic þæt unsōfte ealdre gedīgde
/ wigge under wætere, weorc genēþde / earfoðlīce; ætrihte
wæs / gūð getwǣfed, nymðe mec God scylde* (1655-8). Vergil
often mentions the slight turn of chance which made for the
difference between victory and defeat. Turnus' slaying of Pandarus produces such an effect upon the Trojans that with a
little more vigor the Latins might have decidedly beaten them
(IX, 756-9). So Vergil emphasizes the stratagem of the
wooden horse: *crimine ab uno / disce omnes* (II, 65-6). Turnus refers scornfully to the slender hopes of his foes: *quibus
haec medii fiducia valli / fossarumque morae, leti discrimina
parva, / dant animos* (IX, 142-4). Aeneas hears of their
plight: *tenui discrimine leti / esse suos* (X, 511-12). Cloanthus would have lost the boat race, had he not offered his
opportune prayer: *et fors aequatis cepissent praemia rostris,
/ ni palmas ponto tendens utrasque Cloanthus / fudissetque
preces, divosque in voto vocasset* (V, 232-4). Aeneas nearly
meets his death at the hands of Messapus: *substitit Aeneas et
se collegit in arma / poplite subsidens; apicem tamen incita
summum / hasta tulit summasque excussit vertice cristas*
(XII, 491-3).

Both epics show the heroic spirit of hardihood, the determination to conquer or die, in the face of all odds. So Beowulf expresses his resolve to meet Grendel: *Ic gefremman sceal / eorlīc ellen, oþðe endedæg / on þisse meoduhealle mīnne gebī-dan!* (636-8). In a like spirit he goes forth against the dragon: *Ic mid elne sceall / gold gegangan, oððe gūð nimeð, / feorh-bealu frēcne frēan ēowerne!* (2535-7). The spirited words of Mezentius to his war-horse are in the same tone: *Aut hodie victor spolia illa cruenta / et caput Aeneae referes . . . / . . . aut, aperit si nulla viam vis, / occumbes pariter* (X, 862-5). Pallas thus addresses his enemy Turnus: *Aut spoliis ego iam raptis laudabor opimis, / aut leto insigni; sorti pater aequus utrique est* (X, 449-50). A like desperate courage fires the hearts of the betrayed defenders of Troy, whom Aeneas addresses thus: *moriamur et in media arma ruamus. / Una salus victis, nullam sperare salutem* (II, 353-4).

The hero is appealed to as the ultimate support of the cause he is defending. Hrothgar tells Beowulf that he has never before entrusted Heorot to any other (foreign) defender: *Næfre ic ænegum men ær ālȳfde, / . . . ðrȳþærn Dena būton þē nū ðā* (655-7). In a like vein Hrothgar urges Beowulf to pursue Grendel's dam: *Nū is se rǣd gelang / eft æt þē ānum. . . . sēc gif þū dyrre!* (1376-9). Amata appeals to Turnus as the sole remaining hope of the Latin cause: *spes tu nunc una, senectae / tu requies miserae; decus imperiumque Latini / te penes; in te omnis domus inclinata recumbit* (XII, 57-9). The messenger Saces addresses Turnus thus: *Turne, in te suprema salus* (XII, 653).

The heroes of the epics are not noted for their modesty. Beowulf's first greeting to Hrothgar contains this self-lauda-tion: *hæbbe ic mǣrða fela / ongunnen on geogoþe* (408-9). He emphasizes to Unferth his skill in swimming: *Sōð ic talige, / þæt ic merestrengo māran āhte, / earfeþo on ȳþum, ðonne ǣnig ōþer man* (532-4). He also exults over his slaughter of the nickers: *Breca nǣfre gīt / æt heaðolāce, nē gehwæþer incer, / swā dēorlīce dǣd gefremede / fāgum sweordum* (583-6). His statement immediately following is grotesquely humorous: *nō ic þæs fela gylpe* (586). Before his battle with the fire-drake Beowulf proudly recalls his youthful exploits: *Fela ic on giogoðe gūðrǣsa genæs, / orleghwīla* (2426-7). The heroes of the *Aeneid* are equally loud in trumpeting their own praises. Aeneas thus introduces himself to the huntress on the Libyan coast: *Sum pius Aeneas . . . / . . . fama super aethera notus* (I, 378-9). His consciousness of his own merit is the first thing he mentions in pleading his cause to Evander: *mea me virtus et sancta oracula divûm*, etc. (VIII, 131 *ff.*). Turnus speaks of himself as second to none: *haud ulli veterum virtute secundus* (XI, 441). The boastfulness of the heroes is equalled only by their piety. Little need be said about Aeneas' sense of obligation: the adjective *pius* (which means much more than "pious") is applied to him twenty times; it is applied to other persons individually but three times.[7] Beowulf's trust in God is expressed thus: *Hūru Gēata lēod georne trūwode / mōdgan mægnes, Metodes hyldo* (669-70). Attacked by Grendel, he summons up his divinely given strength: *gimfæste gife, ðē him God sealde, / ond him tō Anwaldan āre gelȳfde, / frōfre ond fultum; ðȳ hē þone fēond ofercwōm* (1271-3). Beowulf explains to himself the dragon's ravage as a punishment for some offense against God which he had unwittingly committed: *wēnde se wīsa, þæt hē Wealdende / ofer ealde riht ēcean Dryhtne / bitre gebulge* (2329-31). A pious boast appears in his last words: *mē wītan ne ðearf Waldend fīra / morðorbealo māga, þonne mīn sceaceð / līf of līce* (2741-3).

---

[7] See too these references to his dutifulness: I, 10, 545; II, 690; III, 480; VI, 403; XI, 292; V, 688.

The hero's personal appearance is striking, beyond that of other men. Aeneas is often mentioned as exceeding his companions (and his foes) in manner and in bodily proportions. So he appears to Dido: *Restitit Aeneas, claraque in luce refulsit, / os umerosque deo similis* (I, 588-9); *ipse ante alios pulcherrimus omnes / infert se socium Aeneas* (IV, 141-2). Vergil at another time applies to him his favorite word *ingens*: *portis sese extulit ingens, / telum immane manu quatiens* (XII, 441-2). (Cf., too, Diomedes' admiring description of Aeneas, XI, 283-91.) The author of the *Beowulf* was at less pains to draw a brilliant portrait of his hero; we may imagine, however, that the complimentary words of the coast-guard are addressed particularly to the leader of the Geats: *Næfre ic māran geseah / eorla ofer eorþan, ðonne is ēower sum, / secg on searwum* (247-9).

The hero identifies himself with the cause of his companions, acting as one of them and sharing their hardships. While his men sleep Aeneas performs the duties of the steersman: *ipse sedens clavumque regit velisque ministrat* (X, 218). When Palinurus is swept overboard it is Aeneas who first perceives the loss of the pilot and rights the vessel: *pater amisso fluitantem errare magistro / sensit et ipse ratem nocturnis rexit in undis* (V, 867-8). He takes a foremost part with his men in preparing the funeral-pyre of Misenus: *Aeneas opera inter talia primus / hortatur socios paribusque accingitur armis* (VI, 183-4). During the passage from Etruria to Latium, Pallas inquires of Aeneas as he would of a skilled sailor: *iam quaerit sidera, opacae / noctis iter*, etc. (X, 161 *ff.*). Beowulf speaks for himself and his companions in his reply to the coast-guard's questions: *Wē synt gumcynnes Gēata lēode*, etc. (260 *ff.*); so he addresses Wulfgar: *Wē synt Higelāces / bēodgenēatas* (342-3). The close bond between Beowulf and his men is suggested by the fact that after the Danes have gone hopelessly away, the Geats watch over the haunted mere, until their leader reappears (1600-5); their return with him to Heorot is thus described: *Ēodon him þā tōgēanes, Gode þancodon, / ðrȳðlīc þegna hēap, þēodnes gefēgon, / þæs þe hī hyne gesundne gesēon mōston* (1626-8).

In Beowulf the King this feeling of community has developed into a larger protectorship, which may be better compared with the feeling of Aeneas toward his people. The Trojan leader, except for his brief and dearly atoned-for relapse at the court of Carthage, is ever conscious of his obligations towards his people and the higher cause of which he is the instrument. (See I, 305 *ff.*; X, 217 *ff.*, 160 *ff.*—instances of his vigilance and forethought.) He is willing to die for his people; thus he addresses Jupiter: *nunc, Pater, et tenues Teucrûm res eripe leto! / Vel tu, quod superest, infesto fulmine Morti, / si mereor, demitte tuaque hic obrue dextra* (V, 690-2). When his ships are overwhelmed in the storm (I, 90 *ff.*), his courage fails; but, as Dryden suggested, his fear "was not for himself, but for his people." (Dedication of the *Aeneid*.) He is not self seeking: *nec mihi regna peto* (XII, 190); his duty is to found a race: *condere Romanam gentem.* He is not a free adventurer, loving war for its own sake. "Énée se bat en héros comme Turnus, mais en héros qui n'aime pas la guerre. Il se bat parce que la guerre lui est imposée."[8] Ilioneus says of Aeneas, *Rex erat Aeneas nobis, quo iustior alter / nec pietate fuit nec bello maior et armis* (I, 544-5). Clearly Aeneas sees in life the conflict between will and desire, and the pathos of the struggle. To him, as to Marcus Aurelius, "life was more of a wrestling-match than a dance." Yet the hero must win in spite of obstacles and must inspire his men when he himself is despondent: "sick with cares" (*curis aeger*, I, 208), Aeneas encourages his weary companions.

[8] Bellessort, *Virgile*, p. 247.

Such is Beowulf's state of mind as he goes forth with his thanes to attack the fire-drake: *Him wæs geōmor sefa* (2419). In his youthful exploits he proved himself to be more than an adventure-seeker, and his altruistic spirit is more clearly evidenced in his rôle as a king. His qualifications for kingship were foreseen by Hrothgar (1850-3). Beowulf's motive for his last combat is not personal glory, but the protection of his people; and his consolation in death is that he has gained for them a great treasure: *Ic ðāra frætwa Frēan ealles ðanc, / . . . þæs ðe ic mōste mīnum lēodum / ær swyltdæge swylc gestrȳnan* (2794-8). The words spoken by his companions after his death are worthy of comparison with Ilioneus' superlative praise of his king: *hē wære wyruldcyninga / manna mildust ond monðwærust, / lēodum līðost ond lofgeornost* (3180-2). Lastly, the hero is attended by a faithful companion: Aeneas by Achates (X, 344; VI, 158; VIII, 466, 521, 586; I, 188, 312), and Beowulf by Wiglaf (2602 *ff.*); he receives counsel from an elderly advisor: Aeneas from Anchises (VI, 851 *ff.*; V, 724 *ff.*), and Nautes (V, 704 *ff.*), Beowulf from Hrothgar (1758-68).

Concept of Fate. The concept of fate in the *Beowulf* is curiously tangled. Whatever we assume the authorship of the poem to be, it is difficult to get any very consistent notion of what the author believed about the control of human destiny. At times God is honored as the dispenser of victory; again Wyrd is named as the director of events; still further, a man's courage and his good sword and armor are held to be the decisive factors. A man may be fated to die and yet forestall his hour of death if he is courageous. The *Aeneid* presents a similar confusion or, we may better say, division of fateful influences operating upon the lives of its characters. Jupiter sometimes assumes the chief rôle as the supreme wielder of destiny; again he divides his power with Fata, as the concepts of God and Wyrd sometimes combine in the *Beowulf*. In the *Aeneid* also there is a margin of safety for the individual, in which much may depend upon his own bravery and resourcefulness. Thus the success and defeat of the characters of both epics seem to depend upon a three-fold set of factors: God or Jupiter, Fata or Wyrd, and individual courage. Sometimes these influences appear to parallel each other; again they run counter to each other and a resultant compromise of their forces brings about the outcome of a given situation. Incongruities in the *Beowulf*-poet's conception of fate are more apparent or have attracted much more attention than has been devoted to the attempt to unify and define Vergil's idea of fate. The Christian element in the Anglo-Saxon epic has aggravated the task of reconciliation by introducing a concept entirely alien to the old Teutonic notion of Wyrd; whereas the inconsistencies in Vergil are at least bounded in the field of a single religion. If we may imagine the *Beowulf*-poet to be familiar with the idea of Fata in the *Aeneid*, a part of the task of reconciling or explaining the whole religious concept in the Old English epic will disappear, for we may say that the tripartite idea of human destiny was carried over from one epic to the other. This shift of opinion may possibly excite more questions than it satisfies, but it at least presents a clue to the solution of the long-vexed problem. The "problem," it may be supposed, did not exist in the mind of the *Beowulf*-poet. The inconsistencies in the Old English epic between the Christian and Teutonic ideas of human destiny are what one would expect to find in a poem which was written by an author who was acquainted with Vergil's loose treatment of affective forces in the lives of his characters, and who assumed a like freedom in displaying the action of God, Wyrd, and individual courage.

The following discussion of parallels will show how closely the two epics agree upon the concept of Fate. The *Beowulf*

represents God as the supreme ruler of events in the following
passages: *him Dryhten forgeaf / wīgspēda gewiofu* (696-7);
mihtig God manna cynnes / wēold wīdeferhð (701-2); *hālig
God / gewēold wīgsigor* (1553-4); *wæs / gūð getwǣfed,
nymðe mec God scylde* (1657-8); *him God ūðe / sigora
Waldend, þæt hē hyne sylfne gewræc* (2874-5). The same
idea is inherent in the lines following: 113-14, 1271-2, 669-
70, 930-1, 1716-17, 1751, 2182, 3054-7, 227, 625-6, 1397-8,
1626-8, 1997-8. Of the 32 times the word *God* is used in the
Beowulf, the deity is mentioned 16 times as the supreme arbiter of human fortunes. Jove is represented in this rôle very
often in the *Aeneid*: in the beginning he assumes the sponsorship of the fortunes of Aeneas (I, 257-60, 278-9); and finally
he provides for the victory of the Trojan by commanding Juno
to desist from aiding Turnus (XII, 800 *ff.*). Other deities
play important parts: (Juno) IX, 745 *ff.*, 764; X, 634 *ff.*,
659-60; I, 50 *ff.* etc.; (Venus) X, 331-2; XII, 786-7; I, 314 *ff.*,
VIII, 370 *ff.*, etc.; (Neptune) II, 610-12; I, 124 *ff.*, etc.; (Juturna) XII, 468 *ff.*, 222 *ff.*, etc. The *Aeneid* begins with the
conflict of gods divided upon the outcome of the hero's fortunes
and ends in the compromise of the warring deities.

Wyrd seems to be the controlling factor in the following references in the *Beowulf*: *Gǣð ā wyrd swā hīo scel!* (455)—cf.
Fata viam invenient (III, 395; X, 113); *him wyrd ne gescrāf
/ hrēð æt hilde* (2574-5)—cf. *fata obstant* (IV, 440), *fas
obstat* (VI, 438); *hīe wyrd forswēop / on Grendles gryre*
(477-8); *hyne wyrd fornam* (1205); *ealle wyrd forswēop*
(2814). The poetic use of *gifeðe* as a substantive with the
verb *ontyhtan* (3085-6) deserves to be closely compared to
line 709 of the Fifth Book of the Aeneid: *fata trahunt retra-
huntque*—cf., too, *unc wyrd getēoð* (2526). *Fata* in the Latin
epic is used 51 times to mean the established rule of human

events.[9] The use of the word *fǣge* ("doomed to die") is in line with the concept of Wyrd in the *Beowulf*: see 846, 1241, 1755, 2141, 2975, 1568, 1527, 2077, 2291 (*unfǣge*), 850 (*dēaðfǣge*). In comparison, Vergil's use of *caducus* may be cited (X, 622); note especially the use of the word in VI, 481, where it means "dead" and the use of *fǣgum* (3025), also meaning "dead." Compare also *fatis debitus* (XI, 759); *Pergama debita* (VIII, 374); *moriturus* (XI, 741; II, 511; IX, 400, 554; X, 881); *moriture* (X, 811); *moritura* (IV, 308, 415, 519, 604; XII, 55, 602).

In line 1056 Wyrd and God are represented in opposition: *wītig God wyrd forstōde*. Thus contrary fates are conceived in the *Aeneid*: *fatis contraria nostris / fata* (VII, 293-4), and Jove's will is at times exerted to retard Fata: e.g. X, 622 *ff*.[10]

Wyrd and God seem to coïncide in lines 2526-7: *swā unc wyrd getēoð, / Metod manna gehwæs*. A similar agreement between Jove and Fata is to be found in the *Aeneid*: *nec Pater omnipotens Troiam, nec fata vetabant / stare* (VIII, 397-8); *fata deusque sinebat* (IV, 651), etc.

Aside from the power of Wyrd and God, the Teutonic hero was dependent upon his own courage. The passage quoted above (1056) continues significantly *ond ðæs mannes mōd*: "God—and the courage of the man—forestalled fate." The same idea appears elsewhere: *Wyrd oft nereð / unfǣgne eorl, þonne his ellen dēah!* (572-3); Beowulf trusts both God and himself: *Hūru Gēata lēod georne trūwode / mōdgan mægnes, Metodes hyldo* (669-70). He owes his life to his armor as well as to God: *him heaðobyrne helpe gefremede / . . . ond hālig God / gewēold wīgsigor* (1552-4). Gummere's comment upon this notion of personal responsibility is in point: "The

<hr />

[9] See John MacInnes, "The Conception of Fata in the Aeneid," *Classical Review*, 24, pp. 169 *ff*.

[10] See Dryden's Preface to his translation, pp. 29-30.

impetuous sense of individual manhood . . . rebelled against this helpless note of acquiescence, and tacked a fiery rider to the wonted phrase."[11]

It is interesting to observe that the "fiery rider" is not lacking in the *Aeneid*. Turnus' brave exhortation to his comrades expresses it in all its ardor: *quod votis optastis, adest, perfringere dextra. / In manibus Mars ipse viris . . . / Audentes fortuna iuvat* (X, 279-84). There are many other passages in the *Aeneid* which stress the importance of the Hero's strength and courage: *vixet, cui vitam deus aut sua dextra dedisset* (XI, 118); *fors et virtus miscentur in unum* (XII, 714); *tu ne cede malis, sed contra audentior ito / quam tua te fortuna sinet* (VI, 95-6); *stat sua cuique dies, breve et irreparabile tempus / omnibus est vitae; sed famam extendere factis, / hoc virtutis opus* (X, 467-9). The last two quotations may well be compared with Beowulf's words: *Ūre ǣghwylc sceal ende gebīdan / worolde līfes; wyrce sē þe mōte / dōmes ǣr dēaþe; þæt bið drihtguman / unlifgendum æfter sēlest* (1386-9). Note also *Dēað bið sēlla / eorla gehwylcum þonne edwītlīf* (2890-1).

Giving of Gifts: War-Gear. Both poems contain frequent references to gift-giving. Generosity is one of the chief qualities of a good ruler. Examples may be seen in the gifts of Helenus and Andromache to Aeneas (III, 464-71, 482-8); Latinus' horses presented to the Trojan embassy (VII, 274-85); Dido's presents to the Trojan fleet (I, 633-6) and to Aeneas (IV, 261-4), and Aeneas' gifts to her (I, 647-55); the various prizes which Aeneas offers to the victors in the games (V, 247-67, 306-14, 351-2, 359-61, 365-7, 535-8; Anchises' presents to Evander (VIII, 166-8), etc. Gift-giving is frequently mentioned in the *Beowulf*: Hrothgar's presents to the hero (1020-49, 1192-8, 1866-7); Beowulf's gift to the boat-ward (1900-3); and his present to Hygd (2172-6), etc.

It is mentioned that the king's gifts are the objects of general admiration; compare I, 709 *mirantur dona Aeneae*, etc., and *Beowulf* 1884-5 *Þā wæs . . . gifu Hrōðgāres / oft geæhted*.

Both epics of course abound in references to swords, armor, and other accoutrements of war. The poets often comment at greater or less length upon the history of some notable weapon; for examples see XII, 90—Turnus' sword; V, 359—Nisus' shield; IX, 303-5—Ascanius' sword; X, 495-9—Pallas' belt, etc.; and from the *Beowulf* 452-5—Beowulf's corslet; 2191-4—his sword; 2610-12—Wiglaf's sword, etc. The weapons are sometimes engraved with historical designs: Aeneas' shield is an outstanding example (VIII, 626-731); cf., too, Pallas' belt (X, 497-8), and the hilt of the giant-sword (1688-93). This hilt also bears the mark of the smith who forged it (1694-8). Klaeber[12] remarks that, although the rune is undoubtedly Teutonic, no other reference to a sword-hilt so marked is made in Anglo-Saxon literature; he says further that the emblems of Vulcan on the shield of Aeneas offer a suggestive parallel. Other trademarks are mentioned in the *Aeneid*: with *Wēlandes geweorc* (455) compare *Didymaonis artes* (V, 359), *exuit ensem / . . . quem fecerat Lycaon* (IX, 303-4), etc. "The bright sword" is commonly mentioned: compare *ensem fulmineum* (IX, 441; IV, 579), *stellatus iaspide fulva / ensis* (IV, 261-2), *aereus ensis* (VII, 743), *ensem auratum* (IX, 303), *fulgentem ensem* (X, 475, 414), and *lēohtan sweorde* (2492), *bunden golde / swurd* (1900-1), *hildelēoman / billa sēlest* (1143-4), *wundenmǣl wrǣttum gebunden* (1531), *beadolēoma* (1523), etc. These last three picturesque substantives are peculiar to the *Beowulf* alone.

[12] *Archiv*, 126, p. 342.

Decorations of the helmet are sometimes specified; the boar-figure is the most common ornament in the *Beowulf*: 1453, 1328, 303, 2152, 1111-12 (?). Compare VII, 785 (chimaera), IX, 50, 270; XII, 89, 493; X, 869; II, 391; VIII, 620; X, 700 (crest). A swine-figure occurs on the shield of Aeneas: VIII, 641. Ornamented shields are described in the *Aeneid*: X, 242; VII, 789, 657-8; X, 261, etc.; compare *fǣtte scyldas* (333), *beorhte randas* (231), *geolwe linde* (2610), *geolorand* (438), etc.

War-horses are described in the *Aeneid*: V, 566-7; IX, 50; XII, 82-4; VII, 276-9, etc. (Compare these lines of the *Beowulf*: 2174-5, 1035-6.) The adjective *fǣtedhlēore* (which occurs in the *Beowulf* only) in this latter passage sustains an interesting comparison with the description of an ornamented bridle in the *Aeneid* V, 310: *equum phaleris insignem.*

Metaphorical Expressions for "Die," "Kill," etc. The *Beowulf*-poet often employs circumlocutory figures of speech to express the meanings "to die," "to kill," etc. These turns of expression are common in the *Aeneid.* Undoubtedly a quasi-religious instinct to avoid the plain statement of these words accounts for these figurative expressions in both poems. Many of these phrases in the *Beowulf* echo Christian sentiments: *fēran on Frēan wǣre* (27); *on ðæs Waldendes wǣre geþolian* (3109); *Drihten sēcean / ond tō Fæder fæþmum freoðo wilnian!* (187-8); *Godes lēoht gecēas* (2469); *gecēas ēcne rǣd* (1201);[13] *on fēonda geweald feor siðian* (808), etc. Many phrases, however, have no Christian connections and savor of the poetic elaboration which is so frequent in the *Aeneid.* References often made to the soul quitting the body may be found in the following passages: *him of hræðre gewāt / sāwol* (2819-20); *hē forð scile / of līchaman lǣded weor-*

<hr />

[13] See Sedgefield's note on line 1201, edition of *Beowulf*, p. 165.

ðan (3176-7), etc.—compare *teque isto corpore solvo* (IV, 703).

Life is again referred to as "given up" or "relinquished": *feorh ālegde* (851); *þis līf ofgeaf* (2251); *ālātan lāndagas* (2591); *oflēt līfdagas* (1622); *hē of ealdre gewāt* (2624), etc.—compare *animam . . . ipse dedissem* (X, 854; XI, 162); *confixi exspirant animas* (XI, 883); *animam hanc effundere* (I, 98); *vomit ille animam* (IX, 349); *animam diffundit* (X. 908), etc. The *Beowulf* contains many phrases which refer to a person "leaving the world" or "going away"—"dying": *worold oflātest* (1183); *grundwong þone ofgyfan* (2588)[14]; *ðū forð scyle / metodsceaft sêon* (1179-80); *fæder ellor hwearf, / . . . of earde* (55-6); *hē on weg hwurfe* (264); *hē āna hwearf* (1714), etc.—compare *superis concessit ab oris* (II, 91); *lucem relinquat* (IV, 452); *lucem relinquo* (X, 855); *invisa relinquam lumina* (XII, 62); *lucem perosi / proiecere animas* (VI, 435-6); *lucem exterrita fugit* (XII, 660); *abrumpere lucem* (IV, 631), etc.

Many of the figures for "die" in the *Beowulf*, as in the *Aeneid*, express a regret for leaving the joys of the present life. Hondscio died remembering the land of the Geats, as Antores died remembering sweet Argos (cf. 691-3 and X, 782). The following examples present interesting parallels: *ðe þis līf ofgeaf / secga seledrēam* (2251-2); *hē dæghwīla gedrogen hæfde, / eorðan wynne* (2726-7); *se herewīsa hleahtor ālegde, / gamen ond glēodrēam* (3020-1); *hē āna hwearf, / . . . mondrēamum from* (1714-15); *gumdrēam ofgeaf* (2469) = *vita . . . fugit indignata sub umbras* (XII, 952; XI, 831); *dulcis vitae exsortes* (VI, 428), etc.

Closely allied with the use of words meaning "to die" are many expressions signifying "to kill." Most interesting is the phrase *under sceadu bregdan* (707), which bears a close rela-

---

[14] See Klaeber's note on the line, edition of *Beowulf*, p. 206.

tion to similar phrases in the *Aeneid*. Klaeber says[15] that "the shades might well be of classical origin." An exact equivalent is to be found in line 25 of the Fourth *Aeneid*: *adigat me . . . ad umbras*. Compare also *quos mitteret umbris* (XI, 81); *ingenti umbra tegit* (X, 541). Vergil frequently uses the word *mittere* to mean "to kill," sometimes alone (XII, 362, 514); again with *umbris* (XI, 81); with *Tartara* (*sub tristia Tartara mittit*, IV, 243; *sub Tartara misi*, VIII, 563, XI, 397; *sub Tartara mittam*, XII, 14; *ad Tartara mittit*, VI, 543); with *Orco* (*miserit Orco*, IX, 785; *demiserit Orco*, IX, 527; *demittimus Orco*, II, 398); with *morti, neci* (*demittit corpora Morti*, X, 662; *demisere neci*, II, 85)—compare also *demittat ad imos* (XII, 884). There are three uses of *sendan* in the *Beowulf* having the meaning "to kill"—a meaning not usual to the word: *sendeþ* (600); *Bealocwealm hafað / . . . onsended* (2265-6); *Hē . . . wearð / . . . forsended* (902-4). For- *sendan* is a word not found elsewhere in Old English poetry. The use of *sendan* and *onsendan* in this peculiar sense in the *Beowulf* may derive from the frequent use of the corresponding verb in the *Aeneid*. By way of enforcing the analogy between *under sceadu bregdan* and *adigat ad umbras*, Vergil's use of *detrudere* may be cited: *Stygias detrusit ad undas* (VII, 773); *detrude . . . sub Tartara* (IX, 496). Compare also *deiecit Leto* (X, 319).

The poetic word *swebban* is used twice in the *Beowulf* to mean "kill": lines 600, 679; compare also *āswefede* (567). Closely related in meaning is the use of *swefan*, "to sleep in death," in lines 1008, 2060, 2746, 2256, 2457. This is paralleled by the fine figure in X, 745-6: *dura quies oculos et ferreus urget / somnus*—compare, too, XII, 309-10. The idea of unlucky or fatal sleep is often repeated in both epics: the defenders of Troy sleep, leaving the city *somno . . . sepultam*

---

15 Notes in his edition of *Beowulf*, p. 150.

(II, 265). Of the Trojans it is said *fusi per moenia Teucri / conticuere; sopor fessos complectitur artus* (II, 252-3). Deiphobus is slain *somno gravatum* (VI, 520). The success of Euryalus and Nisus is partly due to the sleep of the Latins: *Passim somno vinoque per herbam / corpora fusa vident* (IX, 316-17). Rhesus was betrayed in his sleep (I, 470); in her unhappy slumbers Dido saw her murdered husband (I, 355-6); she dreams of the "savage" Aeneas (IV, 465-6); in a dream Aeneas sees Hector's ghost (II, 270 *ff.*); so he is haunted by the spirit of his father (IV, 353). The fine figure of the unhappy dream, to which Turnus' plight is compared (XII, 908 *ff.*), is very close in feeling to lines 1741-44 of the *Beowulf*: *þonne se weard swefeð, / sāwele hyrde; bið se slǣp tō fǣst, / bisgum gebunden, bona swīðe nēah, / sē þe of flānbogan fyrenum scēoteð*. The proud boast of Turnus (XII, 644-5) and the self-sufficiency which he expresses may well find an echo in the words *nō hine wiht dweleð / ādl nē yldo, nē him inwitsorh / on sefan sweorceð, nē gesacu ōhwǣr / ecghete ēoweð, ac him eal worold / wendeð on willan; hē þæt wyrse ne con—, / oð þæt him on innan oferhygda dǣl / weaxeð ond wrīdað* (1735-41). Then the poet continues, *þonne se weard swefeð, / sāwele hyrde; bið se slǣp tō fæst, / bisgum gebunden* (1741-3). Vergil's description is *oculos ubi languida pressit / nocte quies . . . et in mediis conatibus aegri / succidimus; . . . non corpore notae / sufficiunt vires* (XII, 908-12). Who may the "destroyer" in Hrothgar's sermon be?—perhaps the slayer of Turnus. His death is described immediately following the simile; the foe was "exceedingly near" and struck him to the heart: compare *bona swīðe nēah, / sē þe of flānbogan fyrenum scēoteð. / Þonne bið on hreþre under helm drepen / biteran strǣle* with *Cunctanti telum Aeneas fatale coruscat, / sortitus fortunam oculis, et corpore toto / eminus intorquet* (XII, 919-21) and *ferrum adverso*

sub pectore condit / fervidus, (XII, 950-1). The victim
cannot defend himself (*him bebeorgan ne con*, 1746); Turnus
is weaponless, his sword having broken (XII, 740-1). So his
body "falls perishing" (*se līchoma lāne gedrēoseð*, 1754), as
Turnus' limbs fail him (*illi solvuntur frigore membra*, XII,
951). The "unlucky sleep" motif seems to have colored many
passages of the *Beowulf*. So the defenders of Heorot sleep
when the destroyers come: it is said of the warriors who should
hold the hall that they were sleeping (703-4); Grendel seizes
slǣpendne rinc (741); the hall-warders are sleeping when
Grendel's mother comes (1251-2); Grendel's attack on sleeping men is referred to again in line 1581.

Likewise there are in both epics many circumlocutory expressions for "to go," "to march." With words referring to
armor the word *beran* is often employed thus: *hringnet beran*
(2754, 1889); *hiorosercean bær* (2539); *scyldas bǣran*
(2850), etc. This construction is reminiscent of the very
common use of *ferre* with a reflexive pronoun to mean "to
go" (VIII, 199; X, 768; IV, 142; I, 314; III, 599; V, 290;
VI, 879; XI, 762, 779, etc.). Compare also *effert / ora* (V,
368-9); *arma ferunt alii* (XII, 586); *infesta tela tulere*
(V, 582).

Compounds: Kennings. The picturesque sonorous compounds for which Vergil shows an obvious liking furnish a
stylistic parallel to the great number of compound words in
the *Beowulf*, which constitute, it is estimated, about one-
third of the vocabulary of the poem. These Latin compounds
often show a close affinity with the many kennings and other
rhetorical paraphrases in the Anglo-Saxon epic. Following is
a partial list: *velivolus, aliger, armisonus, navifragus, fatidi-
cus, laniger, alipes, fatifer luctificus, nubigena, malifer, armi-
potens, cornipes, corniger, Ignipotens, pacifer, semiferus,
fumifer, armiger, silvicola, aeripes, caelicola, campi salis*

("ocean"), *campi liquentes* ("ocean"),[16] Vergil's compounds having—*ger* ("bearer") as the second element show a close parallel with *helmberend* (2517, 2642), *sāwlberend* (1004—in the *Beowulf* only) and *lindhæbbend* (245, 1402—in the *Beowulf* only). *Armiger* occurs six times in the *Aeneid*: II, 477; V, 255; IX, 564, 648; XI, 32; IX, 330. *Lindhæbbend* and *helmberend* are also reminiscent of *scutatus* (IX, 370), *cristatus* (I, 468), and *clipeatus* (VII, 793).

[16] The possibility that the Old English kennings may derive from classical models is strengthened by the fact that many Latin authors in England showed an especial relish for the decorative value of separate compound words. Aldhelm, for instance, in quoting a verse must stop to remark that it is brachycatalectic, and goes out of his way in the use of *penthemimeris* and *hephthemimeris* merely because they are "beautiful words." (See Ker, *Dark Ages*, p. 34.) A writer like Aldhelm surely would have observed the similarity in the picturesque compounds of the Latin and the vernacular poetry, and in such a writer these stylistic elements would blend.

Chapter V

Parallels in Phraseology

IN ADDITION to the Latinisms in the *Beowulf* which have been discussed in Chapter III, the poem contains many other expressions which savor of Latin style. By way of comparison, reference will be made to the *Aeneid* as often as possible in discussing these examples from the Old English poem; it is believed that some of the constructions cited will furnish more than bases for comparison, that they will encourage the belief that the *Beowulf*-poet was familiar with the *Aeneid* and was weaving into his epic not only turns of phrase but also sentiments which a student of the Latin epic would naturally be expected to admire and tempted to imitate. For the sake of clearness, the list of separate words and phrases will be drawn up in outline form:

Ofersittan. This word is found twice in the *Beowulf* (684, 2528); it does not occur elsewhere in poetry. It looks like a vernacularization of *supersedere*, which has an identical meaning—"to give over, forbear."

Helle hæfton (788). This expression (which occurs in *Juliana*, line 246, and in *Andreas*, line 1342) is, according to Klaeber, the equivalent of *captivus inferni*.[1]

Ealdgewinna (1776). This compound, unique in the *Beowulf*, possibly harks back to the expression *hostis antiquus*.[2]

Forstes bend (1609). This figure of speech suggests a Latin original, e.g. *vincula undarum*.[3]

---

[1] See *Anglia*, 35, p. 254, "Die christlichen elemente im Beowulf."
[2] *ibid.*, pp. 251 ff.
[3] See *Archiv* 126, p. 354.

Gedēð . . . gewealdene (1732). This is a possible equivalent of *subditum facere*.[4]

Morþorbed strêd (2436). This expression (unique in the *Beowulf*) is analogous to the Latin idiom *lectum sternere*.

Ford (568). The ordinary meaning of this Old English word (the meaning which it preserves in modern usage) is "a passage through a shallow body of water, as a river." But *ford* as employed in the *Beowulf* means "sea"—a connotation not found elsewhere in Old English. It is certainly a notable instance, if not a proof of actual imitation, that this word so used, should correspond to Vergil's use of *vadum*, which also commonly means "a passage through a shallow body of water." *Vadum* is used 18 times in the *Aeneid*, however, to express "sea" or "waves of the sea" (X, 303; XI, 628; III, 557; X, 208, 291; I, 112; IX, 713, 670; X, 678; I, 536, 126; III, 706; V, 158, 615, 221; VIII, 91; VII, 24, 198). There are only two uses of the word in the *Aeneid* not meaning "sea." The unusual use of *ford* seems to require an explanation by an influence outside the vernacular; the word *vadum* as employed by Vergil represents a precisely equivalent variation of meaning, that meaning being indeed the almost invariable one found in the *Aeneid*. It seems reasonable to believe that the poetic enlargement of the Old English word may be due to the use of its Latin equivalent in the *Aeneid*.

Gārsecg (49, 515, 537). This compound (meaning "sea") read literally means "spear-man" and suggests Neptune, the trident god, ruler of the ocean.[5] A personification of this nature would not seem unusual to an author who knew several like instances in the *Aeneid*: *Ceres*—"grain" (VIII, 181; VII, 111, 113); *Bacchus*—"wine" (VIII, 181; III, 354); *Volcanus*—"fire" (V, 662; IX, 76; VII, 77; II, 311); *Oceanus*—"sea" (IV, 480; VIII, 589; VII, 101, 226; I, 287,

---

[4] See Klaeber, Glossary to his edition of the *Beowulf*, p. 390.
[5] *ibid.*, p. 314.

745); *Mars*—"war," "courage," etc. (X, 280; VII, 540, 550; XI, 110, 374; XII, 73, 790, 108, 1, 410, 497; XI, 153, 899; II, 440; VI, 165; VII, 582, 603; IX, 766, 518; II, 335; VIII, 495, 676; X, 22, 237); etc. References to Neptune in the *Aeneid* commonly refer to his trident (I, 138, 145; II, 418, 610). He plays an important part in Vergil's epic: he has built and he overturns the walls of Troy (II, 610-12; IX, 144-5); he rescues the wrecked vessels of Aeneas (I, 145-6); he brings the Trojans to Circe's island (VII, 23-4). Frequent mention is made of his worship (II, 201; III, 119; V, 640); even Venus prays to him as the ruler of the power of the sea (V, 778-98). The first use of the word *gārsecg* in the *Beowulf* occurs in the description of Scyld's funeral-ship: "they give him to the sea." The reverential tone of the passage suggests the consigning of the dead hero to the keeping of a deity. The trident-wielding god of the ocean, as represented in the *Aeneid*, may thus be personified in *gārsecg*, which Gummere truly calls "that difficult word."[6] If this connection is possible it should increase our admiration of the poetic qualities of Old English, for *gārsecg* occurs also in prose.

Eftcyme (2896). This poetic word may be a vernacularization of *reditus*, which is found in the *Aeneid* 4 times (II, 17, 118; XI, 54; X, 436). The use of the word in XI, 54 is significantly like the use of *eftcyme*: both words refer to the return of a dead warrior to his home and mourning people—Beowulf to the Geats, Pallas to his father, Evander.

Weorc. This word in the *Beowulf* (like *opus* and *labor* in the *Aeneid*) is characterized by an enlargement or specialization of meaning. It means in the following passages "a deed of courage"—lines 2299, 1569, 1656 ("distress"?), 2096, 827 (*nihtweorc*), 661 (*ellenweorc*), 2835 (*hondgeweorc*);

---

[6] *Germanic Origins*, p. 222.

in lines 1721 and 1638 *weorc* is used to mean "distress" or "difficulty." The word is used three times in a formulary connection with *word* (289, 1833, 1100). There is but one instance of the use of *weorc* simply to mean "task": this is in reference to the building of Heorot (74). Similarly Vergil usually uses *opus* and *labor* to mean something more special than "task." In the following lines *opus* means "a deed of war or courage": X, 792, 469 *virtutis opus;* VIII, 516 *grave Martis opus. Labor* is employed in an analogous sense: XI, 476, 510; XII, 727; II, 385; X, 759 ("distress"?). The use of the words to mean "distress" or "difficulty" may be found in these lines: III, 714; II, 619, 143; I, 330, 597, *Troiae . . . labores;* IX, 225; XII, 177, *tantos . . . perferre labores;* VI, 437, *duros perferre labores;* XII, 33, *quantos . . . patiare labores.* With these last three citations compare *weorc prō-wade / lēodbealo longsum* (1721-2).

Īren (673, 892, 1848, 989, 2586, 1809, 2050, 802, 2683, 2828, 1697, 2259). This word is used in the *Beowulf* only with its poetic meaning "sword."[7] This limitation of meaning is in keeping with Vergil's use of *ferrum*, which in the *Aeneid* is used to mean "sword" 94 times. There are but 12 uses of the word to mean "iron."

Nāthwylc. This word, used as a substantive accompanied by a partitive genitive, derives from *ne wāt* (cf. *ic nāt hwylc*, 274). Its use in lines 1513 (*nīðsele nāthwylcum*), 2053 (*byre nāthwylces*), 2215 (*niðða nāthwylc*), 2223 (*þeow nāt-hwylces*), 2233 (*gumena nāthwylc*) is analogous to *nescio quid.* Compare *nescio quod . . . male numen amicum / confusam eripuit mentem* (II, 735-6).

Bongār (2031). This word (found in the *Beowulf* only) sustains a near relation in meaning to *infensam . . . hastam* (X, 521) and *telis infensis* (IX, 793). Compare also *spicula*

<hr>

[7] See Stjerna, *Essays on Beowulf*, translation by Hall, p. 249.

vertunt / infensi (V, 586-7) and *cornu infensa tetendit* (XI, 859).

Sǣmēþe (325). This brilliant compound (found only in the *Beowulf*) is reminiscent of several phrases in the *Aeneid* which mean "weary from the sea": *senes ac fessas aequore matres* (V, 715); *vada fessis / ... superesse* (V, 615-16); and other similar applications of *fessus*: III, 276, 78, 511, 568, 710, 85; I, 178, 157, 168; V, 41, 29, 717, etc. In this connection may be mentioned *sēoc* (2904); *feorhbennum sēoc* (2740); *heaðosīocum* (2754); *ellensīocne* (2787), which in their meaning, "fatally wounded," sustain a near relation to the following uses of *aeger*: *corpora ... / ... ignibus aegra dedere* (II, 565-6); *attollit in aegrum / se femur* (X, 856-7). The following compounds of *wērig, gūðwērigne* (1586); *fylwērigne* (962); *dēaðwērigne* (2125)—all of which are peculiar to the *Beowulf*—show a close correspondence in meaning to the following uses of *fessus*, not named above: *fessum Dareta* (V, 463); *fessum vasta te caede* (VI, 503). The same meaning appears in *hilde sædne* (2723) and *gewērgad* (2852).

Rūmheort (1799, substantive; 2110, adjective); *rūmne sefan* (278). These combinations of *rūm* (together with *higeþrymmum*, 339, and *sīdne sefan*, 1726) should be compared with the common compound *magnanimus*. This word is applied to Jove in XII, 144, just as in 1726 the reference is to God. It is applied to Aeneas in V, 407, 17; I, 260; IX, 204; X, 771, as the references in 278, 1799, 339 are similarly made to Beowulf, and in 2110 to Hrothgar. *Magnanimus* is also used in an analogous way in the following lines: X, 563, 139; VI, 649, 307; III, 704.

Eoforlīc scionon / ... gehroden golde / ... fȳrheard (303-5). The compound adjective used here is found only in the *Beowulf*. Its use in describing armor is suggestively near to Vergil's use of the expression *auro recocto* (VIII, 624) in his description of the arms of Aeneas.

Andweard (1287). The single use of this word in the *Beowulf* will not allow us to attribute certainly to it a meaning beyond its simplest connotation "opposite." Regarded in its context, however, where an abstract reference to fighting is made, the word may be regarded as carrying the meaning "opposed," "hostile." The word *adversus* is frequently enlarged to denote "hostile": this is the most common meaning of the word in the last six books of the *Aeneid*, where it sometimes occurs as a substantive. (See II, 727; IX, 761, 588, 347, 761; X, 412, 734, 699, 579, 651, 571; XI, 370, 389, 612; XII, 291, 446, 950, 266, 456, 461, 307.)

Wynlēas (1416, 821). This poetic word may be compared with *illaetabilis*, as employed in III, 707 and XII, 619.

Mægenwudu (236); *þrecwudu* (1246). Into both of these compounds (which occur only in the *Beowulf*) may have been carried the mixed meaning expressed in *robur*— "wood," "strength." In VIII, 221 the word means "club"; its use in X, 479-80 closely parallels the use of *mægenwudu*: *Turnus ferro praefixum robur acuto / . . . diu librans iacit.* Compare *þegn Hrōðgāres þrymmum cwehte / mægenwudu* (235-6). Vergil's common use of the adjective *validus* in describing weapons suggests itself as an additional influence in the formation of these Old English compounds: compare *validam vi corripit hastam* (XII, 93) and *validam derexerat hastam* (X, 401); also *validum ensem* (X, 815), *validam bipennem* (XI, 651), *validam securim* (XI, 696).

The meaning of the word *robur* may also be seen in the expression *mægenes Deniga* (155) and *mægenhrēð manna* (445). The latter phrase (which Klaeber translates "flower of men") is unique in the *Beowulf*. An identical use of *robur* is seen in *robora pubis / lecta* (VIII, 518-19). For a like use of *flos* see VIII, 500: *flos veterum . . . virum.*

Drēfan dēop wæter (1904). This use of the verb *drēfan* (translated "cleave" by Cook)[8] is paralleled by numerous poetic uses of equivalent verbs in the *Aeneid*: compare *secat . . . aequora* (V, 218; X, 166); *alta secans* (X, 687); *fluctus secabant* (X, 222; V, 2); *campos salis . . . secabant* (X, 214); *aestum secabant* (VIII, 674); *freta . . . secabat* (X, 147); *secant . . . pontum* (IX, 103); *secant placido aequore silvas* (VIII, 96); *Carpathium . . . secant* (V, 595); *per . . . stagna viam scindens* (X, 765); etc.[9]

Cēol . . . / . . . on lande stōd (1912-13). Cook quotes[10] a parallel from the *Odyssey* which describes how a ship "ran full half her length on the shore" (13:113-15). There is an exactly equivalent figure in the *Aeneid* in the use of the verb *stare*. Compare *stant litore puppes* (III, 277; VI, 901); *stant sale Tyrrheno classes* (VI, 697); *aeratae steterant ad litora prorae* (X, 223).

Cūþe næssas (1912). This expression, indicating sailors' landmarks, sounds like an echo of *nota litora*, which occurs in II, 256 and III, 657. Note also *laeti notae advertuntur harenae* (V, 34) and *nota excedo regione* (II, 737).

[8] *Beowulfian and Odyssean Voyages*, p. 6.

[9] The passage in the *Beowulf* in which *drēfan* is used describes Beowulf's return from Denmark. The poet makes a point of mentioning that there was no wind to turn the vessel from its course: *nō þær wēgflotan wind ofer ȳðum / sīðes getwǣfde* (1907-8). One recalls that upon the three principal stages of his journey Aeneas was beset by adverse winds (departure from Sicily, I, 85 *ff.*; from Crete, III, 194 *ff.*; from Libya, V, 10 *ff.*). Only his last long voyage is peaceful (VII, 7 *ff.*, 23 *ff.*). Perhaps the mention of Beowulf's smooth sailing was prompted by a recollection of the adverse winds against which the Trojan hero had to contend. Cook argues that the return must have lasted twenty-four hours (see *Beowulfian and Odyssean Voyages*, p. 10) and that "this must almost imply that it was near the time of full moon." For a parallel he refers to a passage from the *Odyssey* describing a moonlight voyage. The moon is frequently mentioned in the *Aeneid* in descriptions of nocturnal voyages: see especially VII, 8-9; also II, 255; III, 587, etc.

[10] *op. cit.*, p. 8.

Flotan . . . nīwtyrwydne (294-5). "The new-tarred boat"
is reminiscent of the *uncta carina* of IV, 398 and *uncta . . .
abies* of VIII, 91. The former expression E. F. Taylor translates as "the tarred keel." For a similar note on the latter
quotation see Lejay's *Énéide*, note, p. 627. *Nīwtyrwydne* is
a word found only in the *Beowulf*.

One of the few similes in the *Beowulf* may be noted in connection with these references to the sea. The Hero's ship is
described thus: *Gewāt þā ofer wǣgholm winde gefȳsed / flota
fāmīheals fugle gelīcost* (217-18). Vergil's fine figure (V,
211-16) offers an interesting parallel:

ventisque vocatis,
prona petit maria et pelago decurrit aperto.
Qualis spelunca subito commota columba,
cui domus et dulces latebroso in pumice nidi,
fertur in arva volans, plausumque exterrita pennis
dat tecto ingentem. . . .

Gelīcost is an almost invariable element of the Beowulfian
simile. It is found in lines 218, 727, 985, 1608. The equivalent superlative in the *Aeneid*, *simillimus* (II, 794; VI, 522,
702) followed by the dative may be the original of the figure
in the *Beowulf*, which invariably includes a noun in the dative
case.

Two other similes in the *Beowulf* are reminiscent of figures
in the *Aeneid*. Grendel's eyes are thus described: *him of
ēagum stōd / ligge gelīcost lēoht unfǣger* (726-7). A noteworthy parallel involving the same peculiar use of the verb
"stand" occurs in VI, 300: *stant lumina flammae;* and XII,
101-2; *totoque ardentis ab ore / scintillae absistunt.* Compare
also *ardens oculis* (V, 277); *arsere coruscae / luminibus
flammae* (II, 172-3); *ardentes oculos suffecti . . . igni* (II,
210); *ardentem oculis* (IX, 703); *lux oculis effulsit* (IX,
731); *ardentes oculorum orbes* (XII, 670). The use of the

verb "stand" with "fire" or "light" is also to be noted in the following passages: *lēoht inne stōd* (1570); *brynelēoma stōd* (2313); *lēoma stōd* (2769).

The wasting of Beowulf's sword is portrayed thus: *Þā þæt sweord ongan / wīgbil wanian; þæt wæs wundra sum / þæt hit eal gemealt īse gelīcost* (1605-8). In a like manner the failing of Turnus' sword is described: *mucro, glacies ceu futilis, . . . / dissiluit* (XII, 740-1). The *Beowulf*-poet takes especial pains to describe this phenomenon of the melting sword: in line 1606 he coins the bold compound *hildegicelum*, which may be the *mucro glacies ceu futilis* of the Latin hero. To strengthen the parallel, it may be noted that the hilts are significantly referred to in both poems: Beowulf takes the hilt of his sword back with him (1612-15) in preference to other treasures, and gives it to Hrothgar (1677-8). A long description and history of the hilt follow (1679-98). It is the sight of the hilt that makes Turnus flee after his sword has broken (XII, 733-4). The good swords have never failed before (see 1527-8 and XII, 734, noting the word *ignotum* in the latter passage). Though Beowulf does not blame the sword (1659-60), he should have been wary of it, since it came from the hand of a foe, Unferth. This idea is also a classical superstition (see II, 49). The unprecedented failing of a sword at need is again repeated in the description of Beowulf's fight with the dragon (1460, 2584-6, 2680-2).

Other metaphorical expressions may be noted here:

Scīneð / rodores candel (1571-2); *Woruldcandel scān* (1965); *heofones gim / glād ofer grundas* (2072-3). These figures for "sun" (which contain, it should be noted, the Latin loan-words *candel* and *gim*) are in keeping with similar figures in the *Aeneid*: the eye of the Cyclops is thus compared to the sun, *Phoebeae lampadis instar* (III, 637); the dawn is described thus: *Phoebea lustrabat lampade terras / . . . Aurora*

(IV, 6-7); *lustrabat lampade terras / . . . dies* (VII, 148-9).

Hiorodryncum swealt (2358). This striking compound (found only in the *Beowulf*) is contained in one of the most vivid figures of the entire epic. What the poet exactly meant by it, it is difficult to say; however the phrase *bille gebēaten* immediately following suggests that the idea of sword-strokes is involved. The metaphor is clarified and the borrowing of the *Beowulf*-poet from the *Aeneid* is definitely established if we may regard the following three passages as the originals of the poetic Old English compound: *hasta . . . / . . . alte bibit acta cruorem* (XI, 804-5); *inimicus et hauserit ensis* (II, 600); *huic gladio . . . / . . . latus haurit apertum* (X, 313-14).

Wīgspēda gewiofu (697). This concept of the "weaving" of destiny (probably due in this case to northern influence) sustains at least an interesting parallel to *Parcae fila legunt* (X, 815). Though this is the only passage in the *Aeneid* which refers to the *Parcae* as "weavers of destiny," significant mention of them is made in IX, 107; X, 419; XII, 147, 150; III, 379; V, 798; I, 22.

Wyn with genitive (*hearpan wyn* 2262; *hearpan wynne* 2107; *worolde wynne* 1080; *eorþan wynne* 1730, 2727; *heofones wynne* 1801). These constructions hint of Latin influence; there is a verbal equivalent in *laetitiam dii* (I, 636). The expression *heofones wynne* is reminiscent of other uses of the genitive found in the *Aeneid*. Compare *decus caeli* (IX, 18); *astrorum decus* (IX, 405); *decus Latini* (XII, 58); *decus Italiae* (XI, 508); *decus fluviorum* (XII, 142), etc. The word *Kyningwuldor* (665—unique in the *Beowulf*), seems to carry some resemblance to the poetic expressions cited. Compare also *Troianae gloria gentis* (VI, 767), a trope referring, like the others cited, to an individual.

Godes yrre (711). This expression, applied to Grendel in the context, signifies that he was suffering under God's wrath.

A parallel idea, with verbal equivalence, occurs in XI, 233: *admonet ira deorum*:—the anger of the gods was directed against king Latinus. Note also *ira deorum* (IV, 178), where the same idea is present. Turnus uses the same words with a similar meaning in line 443 of Book XI. *Ira deûm* (III, 215) is a personification: the Harpies are a visible sign of scourges inflicted upon men.

Worolde dǣlas (1732). This use of *dǣl* meaning "region" finds a parallel in the use of *pars* with a genitive in the following passages: *Ausoniae pars* (III, 479); *regni . . . in parte* (IV, 374). See also VI, 440; IX, 790; IV, 153; IX, 1; I, 474; VIII, 433, 682; IX, 521, 691; X, 362; XI, 203; XII, 346.

Eorþan scēata (752); *foldan scēatas* (96). These expressions may be compared with *terrarum . . . orbis* (I, 233); *Europae atque Asiae . . . orbis* (VII, 224).

Foldan bearm (1137); *foldan fæþm* (1393). These figures may be compared to the expression *gremium telluris*. The *Aeneid* contains these examples: *Sternimur . . . gremio telluris* (III, 509); *nec Troiam Ausonios gremio excepisse pigebit* (VII, 233); *tellus / . . . gremio complectitur ossa* (V, 30-1).[11]

Bycgan (1305); *gebycgan* (973, 2481, 3014); *bebycgan* (2799). These rather common words have (with one exception—973) special reference to buying or selling *life*: *ealdre gebohte* (2481); *fēore / bēagas gebohte* (3013-14); *bicgan . . . / frēonda fēorum* (1305-6); *mīne bebohte / frōde feorhlege* (2799-2800). The two uses of the word *emere* in the *Aeneid* (particularly the first quoted below) illustrate the same figurative meaning: *vita bene credat emi . . . honorem* (IX, 206); *optaverit emptum / intactum Pallanta* (X, 503-4). Note also *fratrem Pollux alterna morte redemit* (VI,

---

[11] See Klaeber, Glossary to his edition of the *Beowulf*, p. 282.

121). The use of *sellan* in the same sense may be noted in line 1370 of the *Beowulf*: *hē feorh seleð*.

Higes cunnian (2045). This semi-figurative use of the verb should be compared with a similar application of *temptare*: *animum temptare* (IV, 113); *temptaturum aditus* (IV, 293). Compare other equivalent variants in meaning: *eard ufan cunnode* (1500) with *terras temptare repostas* (III, 364); *temptare latebras* (II, 38); *saxea temptat / limina* (VIII, 231-2). Compare also *sand cunnian* (1426, 1444); *wada cunnedon* (508) with *temptamus viam* (III, 520); *temptare vias* (VIII, 113); *temptanda fuga canit aequora* (II, 176); *temptet . . . aditus* (IX, 67).

Hwetton higerōfne (204); *þīn sefa hwette* (490). The meaning of *hwettan* in line 204, "sharpen" (by words), is analogous to the use of *acuere* in *Quam Juno his acuit verbis* (VII, 330). The second example finds a parallel in *primos acuisse furores* (VII, 406); *acuunt rumoribus iras* (IX, 464); *acuunt stridoribus iras* (XII, 590).

Wordum nǣgde (1318). This expression looks like a vernacularization of *aggredi dictis*. Compare *his vatem aggredior dictis* (III, 358); *talibus aggreditur Venerem Saturnia dictis* (IV, 92); *dictis aggressa sororem* (IV, 476); *aggreditur dictis* (VI, 387). Note also *Anchises . . . ingressus* (VI, 867); *est ingressa Venus* (IV, 107); *invadit* (IV, 265).

Strengum gebǣded (3117). This expression, used to describe the impetus of a weapon, is comparable to *viribus ensis adactus* (IX, 431). The plurals of the abstract nouns used here should be noted. Compare also *validis flexos incurvant viribus arcus* (V, 500); *validis ingentem viribus hastam / . . . contorsit* (II, 50-2); *intorquet summis annixus viribus hastam* (IX, 744); *magnis emittit viribus hastam* (X, 474); *[telum] vi dextera versat* (IX, 747); *validam vi corripit hastam* (XII, 93).

Wordhord onlēac (259); *wordes ord / brēosthord þurh-bræc* (2791-2); *Lēt ðā of brēostum . . . / . . . lēod word ūt faran* (2550-1). These circumlocutions for "speak" find a variety of interesting parallels in the *Aeneid*: *rumpit vocem* (II, 129); *rumpit hanc pectore vocem* (III, 246); *rumpit has imo pectore voces* (XI, 377); *suo rumpebat pectore questus* (IV, 553); *effundit pectore voces* (V, 482); *effundit pectore questus* (V, 780); *effundit pectore dicta* (VII, 292); *fundit preces rex pectore ab imo* (VI, 55); *vox excidit ore* (VI, 686).

Swīgedon ealle (1699). This impressive introduction, coming at the beginning of one of the most striking spoken passages of the poem (Hrothgar's lengthy sermon to Beowulf, the longest single speech in Part One of the epic), is almost inevitably reminiscent of Vergil's *Conticuere omnes* (II, 1), used also to describe the hush which fell over a royal company at the commencement of a long speech, the longest section of transposed narrative in the *Aeneid* (Aeneas' story of his adventures). The similarity of the settings in which the two phrases are placed, and the fact that Old English poetry cannot offer an instance of a similar use of the expression found in the *Beowulf*, strongly suggest the direct carrying over of the Vergilian formula.[12] Compare also other introductory formulae: *Tum facta silentia linguis* (XI, 241)—this stands at the beginning of an important passage: the report of the emissary Venulus to king Latinus—; *deûm domus alta silescit* (X, 101)—introducing the speech of Jove as he expresses to the Olympian deities his attitude towards the Latin war—; *Illi obstipuere silentes* (XI, 120)—before the reply of Drances to Aeneas' proffer of peace.

Swurd nacod (539); *gūðbill . . . / nacod* (2584-5). The "naked sword" (occurring twice in the *Boethius*) is not found

---

[12] See *Archiv*, 126, p. 347.

elsewhere in Old English poetry.[13] Compare *ense . . . nudo* (IX, 548; XI, 711; XII, 306).

Gingæste word (2817). This unusual superlative (meaning "last") is found only in the *Beowulf*. A parallel may be seen in *novissima verba* (IV, 650; VI, 231); *mandata novissima* (XI, 825).

Ārās . . . bī ronde (2538). This description of a warrior on the offense closely parallels *in clipeum assurgat* (XI, 284).

Tō lang ys tō reccenne (2093). This certainly not unusual phrase is reminiscent in its context of I, 372-4:

> *O dea, si prima repetens ab origine pergam,*
> *et vacet annales nostrorum audire laborum,*
> *ante diem clauso componet Vesper Olympo.*

The heroes are describing here their past adventures: Beowulf to Hrothgar; Aeneas to Venus in disguise. A passage in the *Aeneid* just antecedent contains a similar turn of thought: *Longa est iniuria, longae / ambages; sed summa sequar fastigia rerum* (I, 341-2).

Wundor is tō secgan (1724). This may be compared to Vergil's favorite phrase *mirabile dictu* (I, 439; II, 174, 680; III, 26; IV, 182; VII, 64; VIII, 252).

Him on mōd bearn (67) has a parallel in line 39 of the Fourth *Aeneid*: *venit in mentem*.

Him sēo wēn gelēah (2323). This use of *gelēogan* finds a close parallel in the following constructions with *fallere*: *Caci spem custodita fefellit* (VIII, 218); *te sententia fallit* (X, 608).

Cempan gecorone (206); *hē ūsic on herge gecēas* (2638). This connotation of the verb *gecēosan*—"choose" (for war)— is closely akin to the use of *legere* in the *Aeneid*. The participles occur in the following lines: *bello lecta iuventus* (VIII, 606); *lecti iuvenes* (VIII, 179; X, 837); *lecta manus* (X, 294);

13 See *Archiv*, 126, p. 350.

lectae comites (XI, 655); *lectos iuvenes* (V, 729); *robora pubis / lecta* (VIII, 518-19); *lecti*—substantive (I, 518; IX, 146); *viginti lectis* (IX, 48); *lecti proceres* (X, 213); *lectos . . . viros* (XI, 60-1; VI, 73-4); *lectos . . . duces* (VIII, 119-20). (See also VIII, 547-8.)

Mǣton merestrǣta (514); *medostigge mæt* (924); *strǣte / . . . mǣton* (916-17); *mǣton / cūþe strǣte* (1633-4). This use of *metan* is identical with the use of *metiri* and compounds in the *Aeneid*: *iter emensi* (XI, 244; VII, 160); *pelago remenso* (II, 181); *remenso / . . . mari* (III, 143-4); *permensi classibus aequor* (III, 157). Compare also *servata remetior astra* (V, 25); *sidera emensae* (V, 628).

Windgeard weallas (1224). Most editors retain this MS. reading, some (e.g. Chambers) putting a comma after *windgeard*.[14] Klaeber translates *windgeard* to mean "home of the winds." The words taken together are suggestive of *Aeolia*, the *weallas* being paralleled by several words in the following passage:

> *Hic vasto rex Aeolus antro*
> *luctantes ventos tempestatesque sonoras*
> *imperio premit ac vinclis et carcere frenat.*
> *Illi indignantes magno cum murmure montis*
> *circum claustra fremunt.*—I, 52-6.

Strēamas wundon / sund wið sande (212-13). This description of a wave-beaten shore finds several parallels in the *Aeneid*: *exsultant vada atque aestu miscentur harenae* (III, 557); *furit aestus harenis* (I, 107); *miscent se maria et nigrae attolluntur harenae* (IX, 714); *pontus / nunc ruit ad terras . . . / . . . extremamque sinu perfundit harenam* (XI, 624-6).

Se wonna hrefn / fūs ofer fǣgum . . . / earne secgan, hū him æt ǣte spēow / þenden hē wið wulfe wæl rēafode (3024-7). This memorable reference to the carrion animals (cf.

---

[14] See Chambers' edition of *Beowulf*, note on the line, p. 63.

þonne his sunu hangað / *hrefne tō hrōðre,* 2447-8,—in the father's lament for his son) may be compared with two equally striking passages from the *Aeneid*: *terra ignota, canibus data praeda Latinis* / *alitibusque, iaces!* (IX, 485-6)—a lament of a mother for her son; and *alitibus linquere feris aut gurgite mersum* / *unda feret piscesque impasti vulnera lambent* (X, 559-60).

Worolde brūceð (1062); *līfgesceafta . . . brēac* (1953); *līfwynna brēac* (2097). The uses of *brūcan* here to mean "enjoy" parallel a similar use of *uti,* which is represented in the *Aeneid* three times: *melioribus utere fatis* (VI, 546); *utere sorte tua* (XII, 932); *fortuna . . . uti* (IX, 240). All of these expressions signify "profiting by present advantages," "enjoying life's opportunities," etc.

Horn . . . song / *fūslīc fyrdlēoð* (1423-4); *gūðhorn galan* (1432). The "singing horn" of these expressions may be found in the following passages: *rauco strepuerunt cornua cantu* (VIII, 2); *signa canunt* (X, 310); *tuba . . . canit* (V, 113); *Bello dat signum rauca cruentum* / *bucina* (XI, 474-5); *aere ciere viros Martemque accendere cantu* (VI, 165); *pastorale canit signum* (VII, 513).

Swēg ūp āstāg (782); *wæs . . . wōp ūp āhafen* / *micel morgenswēg* (128-9); *Gamen eft āstāh,* / *beorhtode bencswēg* (1160-1). Vergil's favorite word for "sound made by man" is *clamor.* Nearly always accompanying this word is a verb signifying "rise" or "raise"—the meanings involved in *āstīgan* and *āhebban.* As the subject of a verb meaning "rise" *clamor* occurs 15 times in the *Aeneid*: XII, 756, 409, 462; XI, 192, 454, 745, 832; IV, 665; V, 140, 451; IX, 566; II, 313, 338, 488; III, 128. As the object of a verb meaning "raise" *clamor* is found 5 times: II, 222; XI, 622, 878; III, 672; X, 262. The use of the noun in this connection represents a majority of the instances in which it occurs in the nominative and objective cases.

Nō hē on helm losaþ, / nē on foldan fæþm, nē on fyrgen-holt, / nē on gyfenes grund, gā þǣr hē wille! (1392-4). This courageous boast of Beowulf, expressing his determination to seek out the Grendel-kin, is worthy to be compared with Aeneas' taunt addressed to Turnus at bay: *Verte omnes tete in facies et contrahe quidquid / sive animis sive arte vales; opta ardua pennis / astra sequi clausumque cava te condere terra* (XII, 891-3). These Biblical parallels have often been cited: *Psalms* 139, 8-10; 68, 22; *Amos* 9, 2-3. These citations are similar in meaning but exhibit no similarity in situation like that represented by the quotation from the *Aeneid*. The exclamation of Turnus, decoyed from the field of battle by a phantom Aeneas, may also be noted: *quae iam satis ima de-hiscat / terra mihi? Vos o potius miserescite, venti! / In rupes, in saxa . . . / ferte ratem saevisque vadis immittite syrtis* (X, 675-8).

Ne frīn þū æfter sǣlum! Sorh is genīwod, etc. (1322 ff.). Thus Hrothgar replies to Beowulf's morning salutation after the night-raid of Grendel's mother and the death of Aeschere. This speech presents many remarkable similarities to Anchises' reply to Aeneas, inquiring about Marcellus in the world of unborn spirits. Like Beowulf, Aeneas is ignorant of the trag-edy which is bound up in the answer to his question; and the reply of his companion is equally unexpected and solemn. The answer of Anchises may be compared with Hrothgar's reply: *O nate, ingentem luctum ne quaere tuorum* (VI, 868). The almost extravagant praise which Vergil has bestowed upon the adopted heir of Augustus (VI, 869-85) may be seen summar-ized in the direct forceful words of the Danish king: *Swylc scolde eorl wesan, / æþeling ǣrgōd, swylc Æschere wæs!* (1328-9). The stately beauty of the Latin passage (*manibus date lilia plenis*, etc.) is absent from the eulogy of the *Beowulf*-poet; but the solemnity of it and the powerful descriptive touches with which it concludes make it stand out in the poem as prominently as Vergil's elegiac lines in the Latin epic. Both passages bear testimony to the military prowess of the persons mourned: Hrothgar comments on Aeschere's bravery, *ðonne wē on orlege / hafelan weredon, þonne hniton fēþan* (1326-7). This reference to combats of *foot-soldiers* should be compared with the words spoken of Marcellus: *non illi se quisquam impune tulisset / obvius armato, seu cum pedes iret in hostem* (VI, 879-80). Thus it is probable that the famous elegiac passage from Vergil was in the poet's mind as he, in answer to Beowulf's question, put into Hrothgar's mouth this laudatory comment upon the Danish warrior. The differences in the two passages are what we should expect to find in two poems so unlike in general character; the similarities that do exist, if they may be taken as matters of cause and effect, are evidence that the *Beowulf*-poet was not an indiscreet imitator, but a careful judge of his materials and their arrangement.

Ne gefeah hē þǣre fǣhðe (109). This pointed phrase (involving Litotes) is reminiscent of a line in the well-known description of the death and prophecy of Orodes: *nec longum laetabere* (X, 740) and *nec vero Alciden me sum laetatus euntem / accepisse* (VI, 392-3). The passage in Book X contains in the line following the expression *eadem . . . arva tenebis*, meaning "you will die" (*hold* the fields). This unusual use of the verb occurs in the *Beowulf*, lines 1213-14: *Gēata lēode / hrēawīc hēoldon*. Because of the uncommon meaning of the verb, the line has suffered misconstruction; the Geats "held" the battle-field in the sense that their dead bodies covered it.[15] (One recalls in this connection the grim phrase

---

[15] See Klaeber's edition of *Beowulf*, notes, p. 173; *Anglia* 50, pp. 198-9.

which came into being during the World War: a man who fell in France was said to be "a land-holder.") Compare also *campi ingentes ossibus albent* (XII, 36).

Nǣnig heora þōhte, þæt hē þanon scolde /eft eardlufan ǣfre gesēcean, (691-2). This remark of the poet seems somewhat out of place here: the sentiment does not agree with Beowulf's proud introduction and the courageous, almost reckless, attitude he has shown in the Danish court. The "tenderness" of lines 691-3 is Vergilian; the context obviously provides a tempting setting for such a comment, a comment which a writer familiar with Vergil could hardly have foreborne making, even though it were incongruous with the spirit of hardihood which he had just expressed. It may be said further that this reference to death in a foreign country offers a parallel to many passages in the *Aeneid*: the plaint of Sinon *nec mihi iam patriam antiquam spes ulla videndi / nec dulces natos exoptatumque parentem* (II, 137-8); Turnus' exclamation, *Laurentesne iterum muros aut castra videbo?* (X, 671); the poet's comment on Pallas and Lausus, *quis fortuna negarat / in patriam reditus* (X, 435-6); his comment on Antores, *Sternitur infelix alieno vulnere caelumque / aspicit, et dulces moriens reminiscitur Argos* (X, 781-2); and Aeneas' taunt to Anxur, *Non te optima mater / condet humi patrioque onerabit membra sepulcro* (X, 557-8). This last is reminiscent of Beowulf's comment on Aeschere's death: *Nōðer hȳ hine ne mōston, syððan mergen cwōm, / dēaðwērigne Denia lēode / bronde forbærnan, nē on bēl hladan, / lēofne mannan; hīo þæt līc ætbær / fēondes fæðmum under firgenstrēam* (2124-8). The same feeling appears again with double force in Aeneas' lament for Palinurus: *nudus in ignota, Palinure, iacebis harena!* (V, 871).

Stīge nearwe, / enge ānpaðas, uncūð gelād, / neowle næssas, nicorhūsa fela (1409-11). This powerful description should

be compared with Vergil's lines: *tenuis quo semita ducit /
angustaeque ferunt fauces aditusque maligni* (XI, 524-5). In
Klaeber's opinion these verses in the *Beowulf* "can hardly be
explained otherwise than as a case of imitation on the part of
the Anglo-Saxon author."[16]

[16] *Anglia, 50, Beowulfiana,* p. 202.

Chapter VI

Parallels in Motif and Sentiment

THE preceding chapter was concerned chiefly with parallels in phraseology, which, however, occasionally suggested broader comparisons in situation. This chapter will discuss a number of plot-motifs, narrative devices, figurative expressions, etc., in the *Beowulf*, which, reinforced in some cases by verbal similarity, will lay a sounder basis for the belief that these analogies which the poem sustains to the *Aeneid* can hardly be explained as accidental or as common properties of the heroic style, but tend to reveal the indebtedness of the *Beowulf* to the classic epic.

Life in Fire. Common in both epics are descriptions of fire as living. Two of the three uses of *fretan* in the *Beowulf* refer to "eating" fire; *þā sceall brond fretan* (3014); *nū sceal glēd fretan* (3114). A similar figurative usage may be seen in *Līg ealle forswealg* (1122), and in *weaxan wonna lēg* (3115)— upon this use of *weaxan*, Cosijn's opinion was that it means "devour" (cf. *vesci*).[1] These personifications are numerous in the *Aeneid*: *ignis edax* (II, 758); *flammis ambesa . . . / robora* (V, 752-3); *est molles flamma medullas* (IV, 66); [*flamma*] *postibus haesit adesis* (IX, 537); *sub robore vivit / stuppa, vomens tardum fumum lentusque carinas / est vapor* (V, 681-3). The two passages *āstāh / . . . swōgende lēg* (3144-5) and *fornacibus ignis anhelat* (VIII, 421) furnish another specific comparison.

Storm of Weapons. Vergil uses this metaphor in his descriptions of battle scenes more often than any other figure.

---

[1] See Sedgefield's note on the line, edition of *Beowulf*, p. 183.

He probably remembered the storms in his pastorals, which he loved better than the storms of war, and introduced his oft-practised trope into his epic to temper the violence he described. Some of his finest similes contain the device, and again a simple phrase *tempestas telorum ac ferreus imber* (XII, 284) or even the word *tempestas* alone (XI, 423; VII, 223) repeats the figure. The following similes should be quoted:

> *Fundunt simul undique tela*
> *crebra nivis ritu caelumque obtexitur umbra* (XI, 610-11)

> *Furit Aeneas tectusque tenet se.*
> *Ac velut, effusa si quando grandine nimbi*
> *praecipitant, omnis campis diffugit arator,*
> *omnis et agricola, et tuta latet arce viator,*
> *aut amnis ripis aut alti fornice saxi,*
> *dum pluvit in terris, ut possint sole reducto*
> *exercere diem: sic obrutus undique telis*
> *Aeneas nubem belli, dum detonet omnis,*
> *sustinet.* (X, 802-10)

> *pugna aspera surgit:*
> *quantus ab occasu veniens pluvialibus Haedis*
> *verberat imber humum; quam multa grandine nimbi*
> *in vada praecipitant, cum Iuppiter horridus Austris*
> *torquet aquosam hiemem et caelo cava nubila rumpit.*
> (IX, 667-71)

> *Qualis ubi ad terras abrupto sidere nimbus*
> *it mare per medium (miseris, heu! praescia longe*
> *horrescunt corda agricolis; dabit ille ruinas*
> *arboribus stragemque satis; ruet omnia late);*
> *ante volant sonitumque ferunt ad litora venti:*
> *talis in adversos ductor Rhoeteïus hostes*
> *agmen agit.* (XII, 451-7)

Ac veluti montis saxum de vertice praeceps
cum ruit, avulsum vento, seu turbidus imber
proluit aut annis solvit sublapsa vetustas;
fertur in abruptum magno mons improbus actu
exsultatque solo, silvas, armenta, virosque
involvens secum: disiecta per agmina Turnus
sic urbis ruit ad muros.   (XII, 684-90)

The *Beowulf* contains many compounds of *rǣs* (some of them not found elsewhere than in the poem) which repeat the "storm of battle" figure: *gūðrǣs* (1577, 2426, 2991); *heaþorǣs fornam / mihtig meredēor* (557-8); *þū heaðorǣsa . . . dohte* (526). (See also lines 300, 1047.) *Tempestas telorum* may have suggested *ecgþrǣce* (596), a word peculiar to the *Beowulf*; and *īsernscūre* (3116), also unique in the *Beowulf*, looks like a carrying over of *ferreus imber.* A sword is called *scūrheard*—"hard in the storm of battle." Compare also *strǣla storm . . . / scōc ofer scildweall* (3117-18). Is the *scildweall* the classical phalanx, the *legio* of the *Aeneid*? (See IX, 369-70.)

"Surge" of Feeling. Emotion is often referred to in the *Beowulf* as "surging," "seething," etc.—*hreðer inne wēoll* (2113); *brēost innan wēoll* (2331); *him on brēostum bealoniðe wēoll* (2714); *wēoll / sefa wið sorgum* (2599-600); *maga . . . / singāla sēað* (189-90); *mōdceare / sorhwylmum sēað* (1992-3); *Hine sorhwylmas / lemede* (904-5); *heortan sorge / weallinde wǣg* (2463-4); *hē þone brēostwylm forberan* (1877); *cearwylmas cōlran wurðaþ* (282); *weallað wælnīðas, ond him wīflufan / æfter cearwælmum cōlran weorðað* (2065-6). The frequent recurrence of the same figure in the *Aeneid* is significant; Klaeber remarks upon "die ungewöhnliche Vorliebe für dies Bild in der Aeneis wie im Beowulf."[2]

[2] *Archiv*, 126, p. 351.

These passages from the *Aeneid* may be cited: *magno curarum fluctuat aestu* (VIII, 19); *magno irarum fluctuat aestu* (IV, 532); *fluctuat ira intus* (XII, 527); *vario . . . fluctuat aestu* (XII, 486); *vario irarum fluctuat aestu* (IV, 564); *animo nunc huc nunc fluctuat illuc* (X, 680); *aestuat ingens / uno in corde pudor* (XII, 666-7; X, 870-1); *Irarum tantos volvis sub pectore fluctus* (XII, 831); *mens exaestuat ira* (IX, 798).[3]

In a special sense the last two citations made above from the *Beowulf* (282, 2065-6) may be compared to "cool" and "warm" states of feeling expressed in the *Aeneid*. It is doubtful how much of the figurative meaning obtains in Vergil's use of *fervidus, ardeo, accendo, incendo,* etc., in his descriptions of emotion. His use of these words in context both with fire and mental states shows that metaphorical implication, however faint, is to be felt in his application of these terms and others to states of feeling. Out of very many examples of this figure, the following lines may be noted as nearest in meaning to the two citations in the *Beowulf*: *animum inflammavit amore* (IV, 54); *exarsere ignes animo* (II, 575); *spe fervidus ardet* (XII, 325); *urit atrox Iuno* (I, 662); *ardet amans Dido* (IV, 101); *mens . . . ardebat amore* (VIII, 163); *accendam animos* (VII, 550); *ignescunt irae* (IX, 66); *incendere . . . querelis* (IV, 360).

Similarly the participle *gebolgen* and the poetic *bolgenmōd* (1713, 709) suggest comparison with *turbidus* and *tumidus*. The exact metaphorical values of these expressions are hard to determine; the phrase *hē gebolgen wæs* occurs four times in the *Beowulf* as a kind of line-tag (723, 1539, 2220, 2550). Note also *torne gebolgen* (2401) and the participial forms of the word in lines 1431 and 2304. Compare *turbidus ingreditur campum* (X, 763);[4] *adversum se turbidus infert* (XI, 742) and XII, 10, 671; IV, 353; IX, 57; X, 648; XI, 814, for

[3] See *Anglia,* 50, pp. 115-17.
[4] See Lejay's note on the line.

similar uses of *turbidus*. Note also *laetantem animis ac vana
tumentem* (XI, 854); *tumidus novo praecordia regno* (IX,
596); and *tumidus secundo / Marte* (X, 21-2), etc.

The Wounded Deer. The pursued hart to which Hrothgar
refers in his picture of the gloomy lake may be borrowed from
the *Aeneid*. The lines (1368-72) are an obviously studied
effort in description, and a hart in a similar context is not
referred to elsewhere in the poem. The entire passage has
therefore an air of singularity. Upon these lines and their
context Sarrazin remarks: "Man könnte zunächst glauben,
dass diese ganze Schilderung, die dem greisen Danenköenig
Hrothgar in den Mund gelegt ist, nur einen dekorativen
Zweck hatte . . . Indessen ist poetische Landschaftmalerei
sonst nicht im Geschmack altgermanischer Poesie. . . . Der
Hirsch, von dem hier die Rede ist, war offenbar ursprünglich
kein gewöhnliches Wild. Des geht einmal aus dem Zusammen-
hang im Beowulf, sodann noch mehr aus verwandten Sagen
hervor."[5]

Mention of a wounded deer is often and significantly made
in the *Aeneid*. The immediate occasion of the Latin war was
the pursuit of a deer by Ascanius. (See VII, 479-504;—note
the verbal similarity of *heorot hornum trum*, 1369, and *cervus
. . . cornibus ingens*, VII, 483; also that the chase was begun
by hunting dogs: *cervum ardentes agerent*, VII, 481. Compare
hǣðstapa hundum geswenced, 1368.) A wandering herd of
deer is the first sight to greet the eyes of Aeneas, shipwrecked
on the coast of Libya (I, 184-93). Seven of these he slays:
septem ingentia victor / corpora fundat humo (I, 192-3). The
pursued deer are thus described in the royal chase of Aeneas
and Dido: *alia de parte patentes / transmittunt cursu campos
atque agmina cervi / pulverulenta fuga glomerant montesque
relinquunt* (IV, 153-5). The pursuing dogs are mentioned in

[5] *Anglia*, 19, p. 379.

line 132. Two of Vergil's finest similes employ the figure of the stricken deer: Dido is described thus:

> *qualis coniecta cerva sagitta*
> *quam procul incautam nemora inter Cresia fixit*
> *pastor agens telis liquitque volatile ferrum*
> *nescius; illa fuga silvas saltusque peragrat*
> *Dictaeos; haeret lateri letalis harundo.* (IV, 69-73)

The final battle between Aeneas and Turnus is compared to a chase; note that only the hart and the dogs figure here:

> *Inclusum veluti si quando flumine nactus*
> *cervum aut puniceae saeptum formidine pennae,*
> *venator cursu canis et latratibus instat;*
> *ille autem, insidiis et ripa territus alta,*
> *mille fugit refugitque vias; at vividus Umber*
> *haeret hians, iam iamque tenet, similisque tenenti*
> *increpuit malis morsuque elusus inani est.* (XII, 749-55)

Gloomy Natural Description. The passage from which the lines (1368-72) just discussed were taken suggests further interesting comparisons with similar scenes in the *Aeneid.* Although these lines draw a picture which the Anglo-Saxon poet probably did not have to go far to seek, yet Sarrazin's comment upon their unique position in Old English poetry[6] and Klaeber's reference of lines 1409-10, which describe the same scene, to the *Aeneid* XI, 524-5[7] recommend these unusual passages to more narrow inspection. Some of the details in the description—the gloomy water, the "joyless" wood, etc.—are again touched upon in lines 1414-17: *hē fǣringa fyrgen-bēamas / ofer hārne stān hleonian funde, / wynlēasne wudu; wæter under stōd / drēorig ond gedrēfed.* These are the longest descriptions of the homes of the Grendel-kin. Opinion about the location of the haunted mere offers a wide variety

[6] cf. preceding note from *Anglia*, 19, p. 379.
[7] See *Anglia*, 50, p. 202.

of conjecture: some readers believe it to be an arm of the sea; others, a marshy moor-pool.[8] It may be that the lack of agreement as to what kind of lake or swamp we have to deal with indicates that the poet himself did not have in mind a very clear picture of the monsters' home, or else did not attempt to harmonize some incongruous details in his portrayal of it. It impresses one as a piece of description put together from a number of books; possibly there were conflicts in the poet's lay-material. Deep-sea monsters inhabit the mere (1425-30), the "nickers" which the hero slew in his swimming exploit (421-2, 574-5); and yet the idea of an inland pool is sometimes conveyed as in the following passages: *mearcstapa, sē þe mōras hēold, / fen ond fæsten* (103-4); *hēold / mistige mōras* (161-2); *mōras healdan* (1348); *flēon under fenhleoðu* (820); *Ðā cōm of mōre under misthleoþum / Grendel gongan* (710-11); *in fenfreoðo feorh ālegde* (851); *hīo þæt līc ætbær / . . . under firgenstrēam* (2127-8). There is apparent here also a confusion between a swamp and river. To account for the location of the fiends' dwelling in the moors, Lawrence says, "The frequent emphasis upon Grendel's descent from Cain may have led to referring his dwelling to the moors."[9] Bugge comments that, "Hell and the lower world were connected to some extent in the popular imagination with deep or boundless morasses."[10]

The confusion between a morass and a river is what we should expect from a writer who was modeling his picture of the home of evil spirits upon Vergil's description of hell in Book Six. There we have the idea of a swamp in *spelunca alta . . . / . . . tuta lacu nigro nemorumque tenebris* (VI, 237-8), *Stygiam paludem* (VI, 323, 369), *tristis palus ina-*

[8] See Lawrence, "The Haunted Mere in *Beowulf*," *Publications of the Modern Language Association*, 27, pp. 208-45.

[9] *Publications of the Modern Language Association*, 27, p. 229.

[10] *Home of the Eddic Poems*, translated by Schofield, p. lxxiv.

mabilis undae (VI, 438) (compare *Beowulf*, 1415-16); and
yet the idea of a swiftly flowing river is conveyed in these
lines: *Hinc via Tartarei quae fert Acherontis ad undas. / Turbidus hic caeno vastaque voragine gurges / aestuat atque
omnem Cocyto eructat harenam* (VI, 295-7), and the course
of the Styx is described thus: *noviens Styx interfusa coercet*
(VI, 439).

Other parallels may be urged: (1) The underground
river and the marsh (*fyrgenstrēam / under næssa genipu
niþer gewīteð, / flōd under foldan*, 1359-61) are to be
seen in these passages of the *Aeneid*: *qua Saturae iacet atra
palus gelidusque per imas / quaerit iter valles atque in mare
conditur Ufens* (VII, 801-2); *amnem / occultas egisse vias
subter mare* (III, 694-5); *lacu Fluvius se condidit alto / ima
petens* (VIII, 66-7), etc. Compare also Aeneas' apostrophe to
the Tiber: *solo . . . exis*, etc. (VIII, 75 *ff.*). (2) The hint of
the fiery water (*fȳr on flōde*, 1366) is immediately reminiscent of Phlegethon: *rapidus flammis ambit torrentibus amnis
/ Tartareus Phlegethon* (VI, 550-1). (3) The darkness of the
infernal mere (*ellengæst . . . / . . . in þȳstrum bād*, 86-7) may
be taken from Vergil's world of shades: see VI, 268, 340, 404,
450-4, 473, 490, 619, 633, etc. (For other gloomy natural
descriptions see VII, 565-71,—a description of hell-mouth;
XI, 522-5; I, 164-5; VI, 136-9.) (4) The vaguely described
monsters of lines 1425-31 are conceivable as being of the same
brood with the evil creatures of Vergil's underworld: *multa
. . . variarum monstra ferarum*, etc. (VI, 285 *ff.*). The striking lines *Hīe on weg hruron / bitere ond gebolgne* (1430-1)
offer an interesting likeness to the description of these water-
monsters: *angues / incumbunt pelago . . . / pectora quorum
inter fluctus arrecta iubaeque / sanguineae superant undas
. . . / . . . ardentesque oculos suffecti sanguine et igni* (II, 204-
10). (5) The picture of the uprising surge during a storm

(*ȳðgeblond ūp āstīgeð / won tō wolcnum, þonne wind styreþ / lāð gewidru*, 1373-5) is paralleled by several descriptions in the *Aeneid* which refer to a storm mingling sea and sky: *caelum terramque . . . / miscere et tantas . . . tollere moles* (I, 133-4); *sub auras / erigit alternos [fluctus] et sidera verberat unda* (III, 422-3); *maria omnia caelo / miscuit* (V, 790-1); *sese tollit mare, et altius undas / erigit, inde imo consurgit ad aethera fundo* (VII, 529-30); *tellurem effundat in undas / diluvio miscens caelumque in Tartara solvat* (XII, 204-5). (6) The "weeping" heavens (*lyft drysmaþ, / roderas rēotað*, 1375-6) are not without a parallel: cf. *rorantia vidimus astra* (III, 567).

Longing in Absence. The beautiful passage in the *Beowulf* (2444-62) describing the grief of the father for his dead son contains these lines: *Gewīteð þonne on sealman, sorhlēoð gæleð / ān æfter ānum; þūhte him eall tō rūm, / wongas ond wīcstede* (2460-2). They may be compared with the description of Dido's emotion: *sola domo maeret vacua stratisque relictis / incubat. Illum absens absentem auditque videtque* (IV, 82-3). Compare also *Gesyhð sorhcearig on his suna būre / wīnsele wēstne, windge reste / rēte berofene* (2455-7).[11]

The Forced Door. Grendel's entry into Heorot is described thus: *Duru sōna onarn / fȳrbendum fæst, syþðan hē hire folmum æthrān* (721-2). The broken door is again referred to in line 999: *heorras tōhlidene*. These analogous descriptions from the *Aeneid* may be cited: *morantes / impulit ipsa manu portas et cardine verso / belli ferratos rupit Saturnia postes* (VII, 620-2); *limina perrumpit postesque a cardine vellit / aeratos* (II, 480-1); *labat ariete crebro / ianua et emoti procumbunt cardine postes* (II, 492-3). These last two citations are nearer in context; they describe the forcible entry of Priam's palace by Pyrrhus.

---

[11] See *Archiv*, 126, p. 347.

The Broken Truce. Beowulf thus concludes his prophecy of
the resuming of hostilities between the Danes and the Heathobards: *Þonne bioð ābrocene on bā healfe / āðsweord eorla . . .
/ Þȳ ic Heaðo-Beardna hyldo ne telge, / dryhtsibbe dǣl
Denum unfǣcne, / frēondscipe fæstne* (2063-9). This situation—the breaking-out of strife between two foreign peoples
joined temporarily by the marriage of their sovereigns—is
almost precisely paralleled by the disturbances in Libya after
the unlawful marriage of Aeneas and Dido has been announced
by Fama to Iarbas (see IV, 196-7; 320-1). In like manner,
after the "oath-words" have been spoken by Latinus and the
Trojans, hostilities break out which cause war between the
two peoples: Ascanius wounds the pet stag (VII, 483-99),
Almo is slain (531-4), and the Latin war has begun: *stant
belli causae.* Finally, after Latinus and Aeneas have sworn
a truce, during which Aeneas and Turnus shall fight in single
combat (XII, 176-94, 196-215), the war is kindled afresh by
the slaying of a Trojan by Tolumnius (see XII, 266 *ff.*).[12]

A Slain Foe's Weapons Causing Death to the Victor. The
Danish warrior whose death caused the outbreak of the feud
between the Danes and the Heathobards was killed because
he wore the sword and armor of a Heathobard warrior whom
he had slain (see the *Beowulf,* 2032-62). Turnus would have
been spared by Aeneas, had not the Trojan seen on his foe
the armor of the slain Pallas, whom Turnus had despoiled:
*infelix umero cum apparuit alto / balteus et notis fulserunt
cingula bullis / Pallantis pueri, victum quem vulnere Turnus
/ straverat atque umeris inimicum insigne gerebat* (XII, 941-
4). The belongings of a slain enemy were universally re-

---

[12] An interesting parallel in situation may be seen in the characters of
Lavinia and the man who broke into the dragon's hoard. Beowulf's thegn is
mentioned in these terms: *Sē wæs on ðām ðrēate þreottēoða secg, / sē ðæs
orleges ōr onstealde, / hæft hygegiōmor* (2406-8). Thus Vergil describes the
Latin princess: *subvehitur magna matrum regina caterva / . . . iuxtaque comes
Lavinia virgo, / causa mali tanti, oculos deiecta decoros* (XI, 478-80).

garded as unlucky.[13] The incident cited from the *Beowulf*
may worthily be compared to the Aeneas-Troilus situation on
account of its vivid portrayal and its importance in the Ingeld
story.

Epic Tears. Weeping is not plentiful in the *Beowulf*. It is
said that the warriors come *wollentēare* to view their dead
king. This is not overdrawn; but the description of Hrothgar's emotion upon the departure of Beowulf seems to go
beyond the bounds of emotional restraint expected of a Teutonic king (see lines 1870-7). Klaeber remarks of Hrothgar's
weeping: "So scheint dies die Grenze des im germanischen
Heldenepos eigentlich Erlaubten zu überschreiten."[14] The
classical hero was regarded as none the less heroic for copious
weeping: tears flow as frequently as blood in the *Aeneid*.
(These references represent but a small proportion of the
lachrymose scenes that could be cited: III, 599; VI, 699, 1,
213, 476, 686; II, 271, 279; XI, 454, 41, 191, 29; I, 470,
465, 221; IX, 451, 251, 293; X, 842, 465, 790; XI, 59;
VIII, 559.) Zappert inclines to classify Hrothgar with the
weeping heroes of the middle ages, who are the direct descendants of the lachrymose warrior of classical time. He comments thus on the over-use of sentiment in the medieval epic:
"Denn, wenn solche Recken ein Herzleid überkömmt, so wei-
nen sie Kindern gleich, und wir glauben an die Wahrheit
ihres Schmerzes, an die Aufrichtigkeit ihrer Thränen, obwohl
wir uns den in mittelalterlichen Epen damit getriebenen Miss-
brauch nicht verhehlen können."[15] Hrothgar's un-Germanic
emotion may well be a significant mark of the softening influence of the classical tradition upon the Anglo-Saxon epic.
The Danish king's farewell kiss to Beowulf reminds us of

[13] See Fowler, *Death of Turnus*, pp. 155-6.
[14] *Archiv* 126, p. 344.
[15] *Virgils Fortleben im Mittelalter*, p. 11.

Aeneas' farewell to Ascanius: *delibans oscula fatur*, etc., (XII, 434).

Uncertain Fatherhood. It is said of Grendel that no one knew of his father: *nō hīe fæder cunnon, / hwæþer him ǣnig wæs ǣr ācenned / dyrnra gāsta* (1355-57). This same aspersion is cast against Drances, an unfavorable character in the *Aeneid*: *incertum* [*genus*] *de patre ferebat* (XI, 341).[16]

Swimmer's Struggle in the Sea. Beowulf's story of his swimming victory contains some of the finest description in the poem: *Đā wit ætsomne on sǣ wǣron / fīf nihta fyrst, oþ þæt unc flōd tōdrāf, / wado weallende, wedera cealdost, / nīpende niht, ond norþanwind / heaðogrim ondhwearf; hrēo wǣron ȳþa* (544-8); *Lēoht ēastan cōm, / . . . þæt ic sǣnæssas gesēon mihte* (569-71). Palinurus' story of his struggle in the sea is at least an interesting analogy: *Tres Notus hibernas immensa per aequora noctes / vexit me violentus aqua; vix lumine quarto / prospexi Italiam summa sublimis ab unda* (VI, 355-7). Compare the conclusions of the narratives: *Đā mec sǣ oþbær, / flōd æfter faroðe on Finna land, / wadu weallendu* (579-81) and *Nunc me fluctus habet versantque in litore venti* (VI, 362). The narrators also relate how they suffered the attacks of foes: Beowulf sustained the onslaughts of the "sea-deer" (549-69); Palinurus was attacked by his enemies (VI, 359-61).

In conclusion, Beowulf refers to the contest as something more severe than a mere trial of youthful strength,—the impression given at the outset of his narrative in these lines: *Wit þæt gecwǣdon cnihtwesende / ond gebēotedon—wǣron bēgen þā gīt / on geogoðfēore*, etc., (535-7). At the end he says: *Nō ic on niht gefrægn / . . . heardran feohtan, / nē on ēgstrēamum earmran mannon* (575-7). It may be asked: Has Palinurus' narrative lent this darker tone to the conclusion of

---

[16] See Lejay's note on the line.

Beowulf's story? A writer knowing the classic tale could hardly have avoided introducing in a similar narrative something of the sterner feeling expressed by the unfortunate steersman who related the story of his fate to Aeneas in the shadows of Tartarus. The concluding comments in Beowulf's narrative are what one would expect from a poet who knew the Palinurus legend; as they stand, they are out of harmony with the tone of levity with which the story begins: *cnihtwesende* does not agree with *earmran mannon*. The "man more wretched" may be seen in the one bewept by Aeneas at the conclusion of Book V, whose spirit he met *multa maestum . . . in umbra*. (See VI, 340 *ff.*)

Two Men Fighting Under One Shield. When Wiglaf's shield is destroyed by the dragon's breath he fights on under cover of Beowulf's shield: *se maga geonga under his mæges scyld / elne geēode, þā his āgen wæs / glēdum forgrunden* (2675-7). This situation may be paralleled from the *Aeneid*: when Mezentius' shield has been pierced by Aeneas' spear, the Latin takes refuge under the shield of his son Lausus: *dum genitor nati parma protectus abiret, / telaque coniciunt proturbantque eminus hostem / missilibus* (X, 800-2).

Dying Ruler's Survey of Reign. Beowulf's words at his death are not unworthy of comparison with those of Dido, as she reflects upon her career as a queen. Beowulf reviews with just pride his long rule: *Ic ðās lēode hēold / fīftig wintra; næs sē folccyning, / ymbesittendra ǣnig ðāra, / þē mec gūð- winum grētan dorste, / egesan ðéon. Ic on earde bād / mǣl- gesceafta, hēold mīn tela, / ne sōhte searoniðas* (2732-8). A like sentiment is contained in Dido's words: *Vixi, et, quem dederat cursum Fortuna peregi / . . . / urbem praeclaram statui; mea moenia vidi; / ulta virum, poenas inimico a fratre recepi* (IV, 653-6).

Examining Omens. Divination is mentioned but once in the *Beowulf*: *hǣl scēawedon* (204). There is no doubt that this is a genuine Germanic tradition.[17] However, dependence upon divine portents seems to have been of much less significance among the Teutons than among the Romans. The practice is frequently mentioned in the *Aeneid*: III, 222 *ff.;* 537 *ff.;* XII, 247 *ff.;* II, 680 *ff.*, 172-5; V, 525-34; VII, 142-5, 583-4, etc.

Beowulf's Funeral Pyre. The funeral obsequies of the dead king, which form the conclusion of the epic, have given rise to much discussion. According to Knut Stjerna, the account probably consists of two stories loosely connected: a primitive version in which war-harness was burned on the hero's pyre, and a later version in which a hoard of gold was laid in the finished grave-mound after the body was burned.[18] Mr. Chadwick sees in the account of Beowulf's rites "the most detailed description of an early Teutonic funeral which has come down to us, and one of which the accuracy is confirmed in every point by archaeological or contemporary literary evidence."[19] With this opinion Stjerna and Chambers disagree. They say that the custom of burning a collection of armor is not confirmed by literary evidence, and Mr. Chambers pointedly asks regarding the weapons: "Would the pyre have been hung with helmets and byrnies? Whose? Were the thegns asked to sacrifice theirs and go naked into the next fight in honour of their lord? If so, what archaeological authority have we for such a custom in England?"[20] We may well imagine that Beowulf was clad in his own armor when the fire consumed his body; but there was no stricken field with its corpses to supply the war-gear which the poet described as

[17] See Gummere, *Germanic Origins*, pp. 466-70.
[18] See *Essays on Beowulf*, p. 200.
[19] *Heroic Age*, p. 53.
[20] *Beowulf, An Introduction*, p. 354.

burned with him. Evidently the poet had in mind trophies taken from slain foes. These incongruities are set to rights if we may believe that the poet had in mind Vergil's description of Misenus' funeral pyre (VI, 179-235) and the burning of the dead during the truce in the Latin war (XI, 182-212). Mr. Chadwick asks, "Why should he [the poet] lay Beowulf to rest with heathen obsequies, described in all possible detail, when in his dying speeches (vv. 2739 *ff.*, 2794 *ff.*), the hero has been made to express his faith and gratitude to the Almighty?"[21] An answer to this question is suggested if we may regard the poet as a classical student as well as a Christian, using Vergil's elaborate accounts of similar scenes in the *Aeneid*. The Anglo-Saxon author probably felt that in his day the incongruity between classical and Christian tradition was not so great as between Christian and Old Teutonic tradition. So he may have felt that, although his description of Beowulf's funeral-rites was very nearly after the manner of the old heathen practice and therefore inharmonious to the dying speeches of the hero, by imitating the scenes from the *Aeneid* he might plead some poetic justification, at the same time drawing from a source to which he was very near in feeling.

(1) The war equipment is thus described in the *Beowulf*: *helmum behongen, hildebordum, / beorhtum byrnum* (3139-40). The pyres set up at Aeneas' orders were adorned with weapons from the Latin foes: *Hic alii spolia occisis derepta, Latinis / coniciunt igni, galeas ensesque decoros, / frenaque ferventesque rotas; pars munera nota / ipsorum clipeos et non felicia tela* (XI, 193-6). The mound of Misenus was also adorned with weapons: *decorant super fulgentibus armis* (VI, 217). The same question asked above concerning Beowulf's pyre may be repeated here: Whose arms were these on Misenus'

[21] *Heroic Age*, p. 53.

pyre? Apparently a considerable quantity is suggested: evidently they belong to the comrades of Misenus, for they were not taken from foes slain in recent battle. If this sacrifice of valuable war-equipment does seem unexplainable in the Old English epic, we may at least point to a precedent in the *Aeneid*, where the same problem is to be solved. (2) The treasures (*wunden gold . . . / ǣghwæs unrīm*, 3134-5) are also to be seen in Misenus' pyre (*purpureas super vestes, velamina nota, / coniciunt* (VI, 221-2); *congesta cremantur / turea dona, dapes, fuso crateres olivo* (224-5). The richness of the gifts that adorned Beowulf's pyre and his grave-mound is explained if we may see in the poet's description traces of the two well-drawn scenes from the *Aeneid*. Inconsistencies in the setting had to give way before the desire to make the exit of the hero-king a most splendid one. In Zappert's words: "Um einen hohen Begriff von der Schatzesherrlichkeit und Goldmacht ihrer Helden zu geben, bedienen sich unsere Epiker gewisser stehender Hyperbeln."[22] But the hyperbole would seem to be more than an unassisted flight of the imagination; other details in the obsequies are to be paralleled in the *Aeneid*.

(3) Wiglaf, son of Weohstan, had commanded the Geats to collect the bale-wood: *Hēt ðā gebēodan byre Wīhstānes / . . . hæleða monegum, / boldāgendra, þæt hīe bǣlwudu / feorran feredon* (3110-13). These preliminaries are described in considerable detail in Book VI, 176-84; 214-16. Beowulf was next placed on the pyre: *ālegdon ðā tōmiddes mǣrne þēoden / hæleð hīofende, hlāford lēofne* (3141-2). So Misenus was carried forth: *Tum membra toro defleta reponunt, / . . . pars ingenti subiere feretro, / triste ministerium!* (VI, 220-3). Can the *defleta* and the exclamatory *triste ministerium* be seen in *hīofende*? (Compare also *Huc corpora quisque*

suorum / more tulere patrum, XI, 185-6). The fire was then applied. The torch-bearer was pointed out in lines 3124-5: *sum on handa bær / æledlēoman, sē ðe on orde gēong;* but the poet, having described the depositing of the body, says that the *men* lit the bale-wood: *Ongunnon þā on beorge bælfȳra mæst / wīgend weccan* (3143-4). This plurality is to be seen in Vergil's description: *subiectam more parentum / aversi tenuere facem* (VI, 223-4). Compare also *subiectis ignibus atris / conditur in tenebras altum caligine caelum* (XI, 186-7). (4) The body is burned. This is one of the most vivid pictures in the *Beowulf*: *wudurēc āstāh / sweart ofer swioðole, swōgende lēg, / . . . oð þæt hē ðā bānhūs gebrocen hæfde / hāt on hreðre* (3144-8). These lines should be compared to XI, 186-7 (quoted above); note especially the word *ater* applied to fire and the use of *sweart*. Vergil's details were not so clearly drawn in his description of Misenus' cremation: there is no mention of the body burning (see VI, 224-5). The concluding phrase *Heofon rēce swealg* (3155) may be compared to *conditur in tenebras altum caligine caelum* (XI, 187). The lamentation of the woman (possibly Beowulf's queen) mentioned in lines 3150-5 is also referred to in the description of Hnaef's pyre: *Ides gnornode, / geōmrode giddum* (1117-18). This detail is suggested in the description of Palinurus' obsequies: *et circum Iliades crinem de more solutae* (III, 65).

(5) A large grave-mound is then erected on the site of the pyre: *Geworhton ðā Wedra lēode / hlæw on hliðe, sē wæs hēah ond brād*, etc. (3156 ff.). Aeneas did likewise: *At pius Aeneas ingenti mole sepulcrum / imponit* (VI, 232-3). The Latins also erected grave-mounds: *maerentes altum cinerem et confusa ruebant / ossa focis tepidoque onerabant aggere terrae* (XI, 211-12). It is remarkable that the same unusual figure is employed in both poems to refer to the ashes:

bronda lāfe (3160) and *reliquias* (VI, 227). As Beowulf's mound is decorated with treasures, so Misenus' mound is marked with the implements which he had used while living: [*Aeneas*] *imponit sua arma viro, remumque tubamque / monte sub aërio* (VI, 233-4). Beowulf's mound overlooks the sea (2802-8; 3156-8); Misenus' mound was in the same position: *in litore* (VI, 212). (Aeneas also constructed a similar funeral-mound for his nurse Caieta, by which her name was perpetuated: *nunc servat honos sedem tuus, ossaque nomen / Hesperia in magna, si qua est ea gloria, signant* (VII, 3-4). The mound is mentioned in line 6: *aggere composito tumuli* . . . . An ancient funeral-mound is referred to in lines 849-51 of Book XI: *Fuit ingens monte sub alto / regis Dercenni terreno ex aggere bustum / antiqui Laurentis.*)

(6) In conclusion, the *Beowulf*-poet describes how the warriors ride around the mound, praising the virtues of the dead hero. Twelve warriors pass about Beowulf's tomb: *Þā ymbe hlǣw riodan hildedēore, / æþelinga bearn, ealra twelfe, / woldon care cwīðan, ond kyning mǣnan*, etc., (3169 ff.). So the priest passes around the sepulchre of Misenus: *Idem ter socios pura circumtulit unda* (VI, 229). Likewise the Trojans ride about the pyres of their comrades: *ter circum accensos . . . / decurrere rogos, ter maestum funeris ignem/lustravere in equis ululatusque ore dedere* (XI, 188-90). Compare too *Swā begnornodon Gēata lēode/hlāfordes hryre* (3178-9). (7) The mounds stand as perpetual memorials to the fame of the hero. Beowulf commanded his grave-mound with a view to his future renown: *Hātað heaðomǣre hlǣw gewyrcean/ . . . sē scel tō gemyndum mīnum lēodum/hēah hlīfian on Hronesnæsse, / þæt hit sǣlīðend syððan hātan / Bīowulfes biorh* (2802-7). A similar comment closes the description of Misenus' rites: of his mound it is said *nunc Misenus ab illo/dicitur aeternumque tenet per saecula nomen* (VI, 234-5). Polydorus

is remembered by the same kind of monument: *instauramus Polydoro funus et ingens/aggeritur tumulo tellus* (III, 62-3). Aeneas reports to Palinurus, whom he finds in the Underworld, that his name is thus remembered: *statuent tumulum et tumulo sollemnia mittent,/aeternumque locus Palinuri nomen habebit* (VI, 380-1).

The bale-fire of Hnaef and Hildeburh's two sons (1107-24) deserves some additional comment. Of this double cremation and burial, Stjerna remarks that it "lacks archaeological parallels in northern Europe."[23] But this is precisely the situation in Book XI of the *Aeneid*, which also took place after a cessation of hostilities and on the battlefield where the cremated warriors had fallen. The Trojans burned their dead *en masse* (XI, 185-96, already quoted); of the Latins it is said *cetera confusaeque ingentem caedis acervum/ . . . cremant* (XI, 207-8). In comparison with the details noted from Beowulf's pyre and from that of Misenus and the armies in Book XI, it should be observed that Hnaef and his companions were burned in their armor: *swātfāh syrce, swȳn ealgylden,/eofer īrenheard*, etc. (1111 *ff.*); the weeping of women is mentioned (1117-18); the fire is described: *Wand tō wolcnum wælfȳra mǣst,/hlynode for hlāwe* (1119-20); and the burning bodies are vividly pictured: *hafelan multon*, etc. (1120 *ff.*).

Beowulf—Unferth: Turnus—Drances. The verbal encounter of Beowulf and Unferth is out of accord with the situation in which it occurs. Here is an honored guest of a king insulted by an envious cowardly thane in the presence of the royal company of friends and strangers assembled in Heorot, which the hero has just volunteered to defend at the risk of his life. This battle of wits is not the primitive flyting or song-contest; it is more serious. Gummere says of the episode: "It is rather a report of the spirited way in which Beowulf carried off the laurels

[23] *Essays on Beowulf*, p. 171.

in the 'hazing' of the guest by a competent official of the host; but it seems a strange survival in the epic by the side of the courtly and extravagant compliments exchanged between Beowulf and Hrothgar."[24] The incongruity of the situation the poet has apparently attempted to soften by the fine rhetoric of Beowulf's reply (530-607), which is certainly one of the best speeches in the poem. This same attempt on the part of the author may be seen in the later exchange of compliments between the foes: in his remark on Unferth's loan of his sword as Beowulf prepares for the conflict with Grendel's dam (1455-72) and the hero's courteous mention of it and its owner (1488-90) and on two later occasions (1659-60, 1807-12). The matters enacted between Beowulf and Unferth, taken in sum, contain nothing therefore of the hostility and coarseness to be found in similar passages in other northern poems (in the *Lokasenna*, for instance) and the cases reported by Saxo. Thus the poet has refined his scene to something of a gentlemen's quarrel; but the question remains: Why should he have introduced it at all, since it is so incongruous to the events which came before and after it? An answer may be sought in the fine episode in the Eleventh Book of the *Aeneid*, where the character of the hero Turnus is shown in his noble reply to the taunts of the trouble-maker Drances. This scene may well have been a temptation to the *Beowulf*-poet, for it undoubtedly is one of the most dramatic passages of the *Aeneid* and presents a hero after the style of the true Teutonic order: a man skilful in words and ready to back them up with his sword at any odds.[25]

These parallels in situation are worthy of notice: (1) The trouble-maker speaks against a trusted champion of his king; Hrothgar has expressed his confidence in Beowulf (375-89); Turnus is the proclaimed leader of the forces of Latinus (VII, 783 ff., 595 ff., etc.). (2) He is known as an envious person.

---

[24] *The Oldest English Epic*, p. 45.
[25] See *Archiv*, CXXVI, pp. 340-1.

It is said of Unferth *wæs him Bēowulfes sīð,/mōdges mere-faran, micel æfþunca,/forþon þe hē ne ūþe, þæt ǣnig ōðer man/æfre mǣrða þon mā middangeardes/gehēde under heofe-num þonne hē sylfa* (501-5). Drances feels the same jealousy of Turnus: *quem gloria Turni/obliqua invidia stimulisque agi-tabat amaris* (XI, 336-7). (3) He bears a shady reputation in other respects. Beowulf casts this reproach at Unferth: *ðū þīnum brōðrum tō banan wurde;/ . . . . þæs þū in helle scealt/ werhðo drēogan, þēah þīn wit duge* (587-9). The poet repeats this dark hint: *hē his māgum nǣre/ārfæst æt ecga gelācum* (1167-8). Drances is a traitor on a somewhat larger scale: he extravagantly lauds the enemy of his country and advises com-position with him (XI, 124-31). He is said to be a bad patriot: *odiis et crimine Drances/ infensus iuveni Turno* (XI, 122-3); he is again called *seditione potens* (XI, 340). Turnus warns him not to praise the enemies of Latium, *extollere viros/gentis bis victae* (XI, 401-2). Did the poet have these hints of larger villainy in mind when he said of Unferth, sitting at the feet of his king, that everyone trusted him even though he had not dealt fairly with his own family? (4) He taunts the hero to action. Unferth thus casts his slur at Beowulf: *Ðonne wēne ic tō þē wyrsan geþingea,/ðēah þū heaðorǣsa gehwǣr dohte,/ grimre gūðe, gif þū Grendles dearst/nihtlongne fyrst nēan bīdan* (525-8). Drances urges Turnus to attack Aeneas: *Aut, si fama movet, si tantum pectore robur/concipis, . . . /aude atque adversum fidens fer pectus in hostem* (XI, 368-70); *Etiam tu, si qua tibi vis,/ si patrii quid Martis habes, illum aspice contra,/qui vocat* (XI, 373-5). (5) The hero begins his reply by rallying his antagonist for his long speech. Beowulf thus addresses Unferth: *Hwæt, þū worn fela, wine mīn Un-ferð, / . . . ymb Brecan sprǣce, / sægdest from his sīðe* (530-2). Turnus says to Drances, *Larga quidem, Drance, sem-per tibi copia fandi* (XI, 378). (6) The hero upbraids his antagonist for cowardice. Having given his version of the swimming-contest, Beowulf says pointedly to Unferth: *Nō ic wiht fram þē/swylcra searonīða secgan hȳrde,/billa brōgan* (581-3). Turnus refers ironically to Drances' exploits which never were: *Proinde tona eloquio (solitum tibi) meque timoris/ argue tu, Drance, quando tot stragis acervos/Teucrorum tua dextra dedit passimque tropaeis/insignis agros* (XI, 383-6).

(7) The hero then refers directly to the danger at hand and challenges his antagonist to dare it. Beowulf taunts Unferth by saying that his deeds do not match his words: *Secge ic þē tō sōðe, sunu Ecglāfes, þæt næfre Grendel swā fela gryra gefremede, / . . . gif þīn hige wǣre, / sefa swā searogrim swā þū self talast* (590-4). Turnus is equally as plain spoken to Drances: *Possit quid vivida virtus / experiare licet nec longe scilicet hostes / quaerendi nobis: circumstant undique muros. / Imus in adversos? Quid cessas? an tibi Mavors / ventosa in lingua pedibusque fugacibus istis / semper erit?* (XI, 386-91). Neither do the poets themselves spare the heroes' antagonists: when Unferth hands over his sword to Beowulf the poet says he gives it to "a better warrior" and remarks further: *selfa ne dorste / under ȳða gewin aldre genēþan, / drihtscype drēogan; þǣr hē dōme forlēas, / ellenmǣrðum* (1468-71). Vergil says of Drances that he was a skilful talker, *sed frigida bello / dextera* (XI, 338-9). (8) The hero answers the insinuations of his opponent by giving his own account of his exploits. Beowulf tells of his superiority over Breca, his slaying of the sea-monsters, and his struggle with the waves (535-81). Turnus recounts his prowess in the Latin war: *Pulsus ego? aut quisquam merito . . . pulsum / arguet, Iliaco tumidum qui crescere Thybrim / sanguine et Evandri totam cum stirpe videbit / procubuisse domum atque exutos Arcadas armis? / Haud ita me experti Bitias et Pandarus ingens / et quos mille die victos sub Tartara misi, / inclusus muris*

hostilique aggere saeptus (XI, 392-8). (9) The hero repeats his determination to go forward into the present danger. Beowulf says confidently, *Ac ic him Gēata sceal / eafoð ond ellen ungeāra nū, / gūþe gebēodan* (601-3). The remainder of Turnus' lengthy speech (XI, 378-444) is in the same vein and might well be summarized by Beowulf's succinct remark just quoted. He says he is confident of the strength of his Latin allies and is willing to meet his chief foe in single combat: *Ibo animis contra, vel magnum praestet Achillem / factaque Vulcani manibus paria induat arma / ille licet!* (XI, 438-40). Some of Turnus' remarks are reminiscent of other parts of Beowulf's speeches: he refers to the fortune of war, *Multa dies variique labor mutabilis aevi / rettulit in melius; multos alterna revisens / lusit et in solido rursus Fortuna locavit* (XI, 425-7). Compare Beowulf's *Gǣð ā wyrd swā hīo scel* (455). Turnus declares his devotion to the Latin people: *Vobis animam hanc soceroque Latino, / Turnus ego, haud ulli veterum virtute secundus, / devovi* (XI, 440-2). In a like spirit Beowulf proclaims his devotion to the Danes: *Ic þæt hogode . . . / þæt ic ānunga ēowra lēoda / willan geworhte, opðe on wæl crunge* (632-5). It is interesting to remember that, later, in the stress of battle the hero "remembers his boast" and is spurred on to greater efforts. As the battle begins to turn against him, Turnus cries *dextra nec Drancis dicta refellam!* (XII, 644). Beowulf under the clutch of Grendel recalls his boast: *Gemunde þā se gōda . . . / ǣfensprǣce, ūplang āstōd / ond him fæste wiðfēng* (758-60).

Cain and Grendel: The Hydra. The Grendel-brood are undoubtedly pagan in origin, connected by Hebrew and Christian tradition with Cain and his infernal descendants.[26] In the *Beowulf* Grendel is said to be the offspring of Cain and

[26] See Kennedy, *The Caedmon Poems*, p. xlvii; Lawrence, *Beowulf and Epic Tradition*, pp. 161-2; Paul und Braune, *Beiträge*, xiii, pp. 210.

shares his punishment (1261-6; 106-14). He is probably the
Hydra of the Sixth Book of the *Aeneid*, "one of the unknown,
pre-Beowulfian sources of the poem, associated with Cain."[27]
This identification is very natural, as the Church fathers had
frequently cited Cain and the Hydra to symbolize heretics.
Of this tradition the *Beowulf*-poet was undoubtedly aware:
and Vergil's description of the Hydra as a monster of Hades
together with other defeated enemies of Jove would have
agreed with the idea of Cain's punishment, and furthermore
would have inspired the poet in painting the horrors of the
uncanny home of the Grendel-kin, which, as has been seen,
seems to be touched with the dark colors of Vergil's Tartarus.
The Hydra of VI, 576-7 (*quinquaginta atris immanis hiati-
bus Hydra / saevior intus habet sedem*) is not the *belua
Lernae* of line 287, which is also described in VII, 658, and
VIII, 300. Whether or not the two hydras, both inmates of
hell, were regarded as separate monsters, the Hydra of VI,
576-7 has the satisfying proportions which would have interested a writer capable of describing the fire-dragon in the
second part of the *Beowulf;* and this Hydra is undoubtedly
the monster which Mr. Hagen believes to be identical with
Grendel.[28]

*The Beowulf—Grendel Story and the Hercules—Cacus
Story.* These important episodes show many significant resemblances: (1) Grendel and Cacus wreak wholesale ravage
upon an entire people over a long period of time (compare
274-7, 473-8, 146-9, 1577-84 and VIII, 195-7). (2) They
are half-human, of monstrous size; Grendel is spoken of as
a "man" (*wer*, 105), but is not of mortal kind: *hē wæs māra
þonne ǣniᵹ man ōðer* (1353). Cacus is thus described: *magna
se mole ferebat* (VIII, 199), and the words *semihomo* and

---

[27] J. E. Routh, *Ballad Theory of the Beowulf*, p. 26.
[28] See *Modern Language Notes*, XIX, 72.

semiferus are applied to him (VIII, 194, 267). The reader of the *Beowulf* has difficulty in imagining what Grendel looked like. There is no clear impression: many details and half-hints in the poem are hard to reconcile. One feels that the author had no very clear idea of the monster's appearance. The question may be raised: Was he hesitating between the *semihomo* and the *semiferus* of Vergil's vague description of Cacus? (3) The monsters inhabit deep homes of darkness. Nothing further in this connection need be said about the Grendel-mere. Cacus' dwelling is a gloomy cave: *Hic spelunca fuit, vasto submota recessu* (VIII, 193); it is inaccessible to the rays of the sun, a vast region of darkness, *umbrosae penitus patuere cavernae* (VIII, 242—see also VIII, 195). It takes a day for Beowulf to reach the monster's cavern through the water (1495-6). Grendel is first referred to as *sē þe in þýstrum bād* (87). (4) Their homes are surrounded by uncanny monsters: see the *Beowulf* 1425-31. Evil birds live near Cacus' cave: *dirarum nidis domus opportuna volucrum* (VIII, 235); it extends to the depths occupied by the fiends of hell: *penitus vi terra dehiscens / infernas reseret sedes et regna recludat / pallida, dis invisa, . . . / . . . trepident immisso lumine Manes* (VIII, 243-6). (5) The heroes are regarded as divinely sent. Hrothgar says of Beowulf *Hine hālig God / for ārstafum ūs onsende* (381-2). Compare Evander's comment upon Hercules: *attulit et nobis aliquando optantibus aetas / auxilium adventumque dei* (VIII, 200-1). Hercules is described throughout Evander's story as in his usual character of a champion of civilization. Thus Beowulf fights for man against beasts; in a larger sense he may be regarded as symbolizing the spirit of humanity, combating the violence of destructive natural forces, represented by the Grendel-brood.

(6) The heroes arrive fresh from recent victories. Beowulf has conquered giants and nickers (420-2); Hercules' arrival is thus described: *maximus ultor/tergemini nece Geryonae spoli-*

isque superbus/Alcides aderat . . . victor (VIII, 201-3). (7) The heroes use the same method to slay the monsters: their hand-grip. Beowulf's grip is famous:[29] Hrothgar mentions it in lines 379-81. We may suppose that the hero employed it in his victory over the giants (420); and he makes a point of saying that he will use it against Grendel: *ic mid grāpe sceal / fōn wið fēonde* (438-9). He tears off Grendel's arm by main force (760-5, 815-18), and stresses this feat in his account to Hrothgar (963-72). Beowulf also grapples with Grendel's dam (*strenge getrūwọde, / mundgripe mægenes*, 1533-4), and uses the giant-sword as a last recourse. The other attributes of the courageous Geatish hero require that we see in his gift of strength something more than a bearish trait; surely it is more like the grip of Hercules. By this means Hercules slew Cacus: *Hic Cacum in tenebris . . . / corripit in nodum com-plexus, et angit inhaerens / elisos oculos et siccum sanguine guttur* (VIII, 259-61). The characters of Beowulf and Hercules as benefactors of civilization add an important element to the epics in which they play their parts. Hercules' feat is in keeping with the general tone of the *Aeneid*: "There remains the view to which many critics have lent their support, that the *Aeneid* celebrates the triumph of law and civilization over the savage instincts of man."[30] Earle[31] sees a similar motif in the Anglo-Saxon epic: "The general sense of the poem is this: there is work for the age of blood and iron but such an age must yield to a better. Force is not the supreme and final arbiter of human destiny; above and behind Might is enthroned the diviner

---

[29] Beowulf's grip is mentioned elsewhere in the poem: it is his favorite method of combat. Thus he slew Daeghrefn: *ne wæs ecg bona, / ac him hilde-grāp heortan wylmas, / bānhūs gebræc* (2506-8). He regrets that he must use a sword against the fire-drake (2518-22). This means of offense is to be found in the *Aeneid* XI, 743-4: *dereptum ab equo dextra complectitur hostem / et grem-ium ante suum multa vi concitus aufert.*

[30] Cruttwell, *History of Roman Literature*, p. 269.

[31] *Deeds of Beowulf*, p. lxxxviii.

genius of Right. In this idea we recognize the essential thought of Civilization, the clue to emergence out of barbarism."

(8) It is said that the monsters, attacked by the heroes, show fear, contrary to their former boldness. Grendel's terror is thus expressed: *Hyge wæs him hinfūs, wolde on heolster flēon, / sēcan dēofla gedræg; ne wæs his drohtoð þær / swylce hē on ealderdagum ær gemētte* (755-7). He seeks his home: *scolde Grendel þonan / . . . flêon under fenhleoðu, / sēcean wynlēas wīc* (819-21). So Cacus seeks to escape: *Tum primum nostri Cacum videre timentem / turbatumque oculis; fugit ilicet ocior Euro / speluncamque petit: pedibus timor addidit alas* (VIII, 222-4). (9) The dead monsters are exposed to the general view. Grendel's head is brought into Heorot: *þā wæs be feaxe on flet boren / Grendles hēafod, þær guman druncon, / egeslīc for eorlum ond þære idese mid, / wliteseon wrǣtlīc; weras on sāwon* (1647-50). This mention of the woman in the company is a delicate touch: it implies a sensitiveness in the poet akin to "Vergilian tenderness." So Evander's folk view the horrible corpse of Cacus: *pedibus informe cadaver/protrahitur. Nequeunt expleri corda tuendo / terribiles oculos, vultum villosaque saetis / pectora semiferi, atque exstinctos faucibus ignes* (VIII, 264-7).[32] (10) The victorious heroes are perpetually honored by a grateful people. After the encounter with Grendel, Beowulf's praise is recited by a court minstrel (867-74). Hrothgar praises him thus: *Þū þē self hafast / dǣdum*

---

[32] These descriptions of monsters offer interesting parallels: The fire-drake (*mid bǣle fōr / fȳre gefȳsed*, etc., 2308 ff.) compares well in some respects with Cacus: *glomerat sub antro / fumiferam noctem, commixtis igne tenebris* (VIII, 254-5). Compare also the monster described in Book X, 565-7: *centum cui bracchia dicunt / centenasque manus, quinquaginta oribus ignem / pectoribusque arsisse.* The fire-drake as a night-flier is reminiscent of Fama described in IV, 184-7: *Nocte volat caeli medio terraeque, per umbram / stridens, . . . / . . . et magnas territat urbes;* compare *æfter lyfte lācende hwearf / middelnihtum, māðmǣhta wlonc / ansȳn ȳwde* (2832-4). Grendel's hand and arm triumphantly displayed on Heorot (983-7) remind one of the *uncae manus* (III, 217) of the predatory Harpies: *pedibus circumvolat uncis* (III, 233).

gefremed, þæt þīn dōm lyfað / āwa tō aldre (953-5). Similarly
Wealhtheow addresses him: *Hafast þū gefēred, þæt ðē feor
ond nēah / ealne wīdeferhþ weras ehtigað, / efne swā sīde swā
sǣ bebūgeð / windgeard weallas* (1221-4). In his farewell sermon Hrothgar says, *Blǣd is ārǣred / geond wīdwegas, wine
mīn Bēowulf, / ðīn ofer þēoda gehwylce* (1703-5). Like honors
were bestowed on Hercules immediately after his defeat of
Cacus: *Ex illo celebratus honos,* etc. (VIII, 268 *ff.*)

Hrothgar: Evander, Latinus. As the model of an aged benefi-
cent ruler, Hrothgar represents many qualities which suggest that the two elderly kings of the *Aeneid* may have lent
something of their characters to his. Several details of the
action in which these personages play their parts are strikingly
similar. (1) As Beowulf and his man approach the palace of
Hrothgar, they are required to answer the coast-guard's questions about their origin, intention, etc. (237-40, 254-7). So
Pallas, the son of Evander, interrogates Aeneas: *Iuvenes, quae
causa subegit / ignotas temptare vias? quo tenditis? . . . / Qui
genus? unde domo? pacemne huc fertis an arma?* (VIII, 112-
14). Latinus asks the Trojans similar questions: *Dicite, Dar-
danidae . . . / quid petitis? quae causa rates aut cuius egen-
tes / litus ad Ausonium tot per vada caerula vexit?* (VII,
195-8). (2) As Beowulf is kindly welcomed by the coast-guard
and invited to proceed, as soon as his mission is told (291-4,
316-18), so Aeneas and his troop are greeted by Pallas as soon
as the youth hears the name of the visitor: *'Egredere, o quicum-
que es,' ait, 'coramque parentem / alloquere ac nostris succede
Penatibus hospes'* (VIII, 122-3). Compare Wulfgar's invitation to Beowulf: *Nū gē mōton gangan in ēowrum gūðsear-
wum / . . . Hrōðgār gesēon* (395-6). (3) The kings are
familiar with the antecedents of the newcomers and make mention of their family-histories. Hrothgar refers to Beowulf's
father (372-6, 459-72); Evander says to Aeneas, *Ut verba
parentis / et vocem Anchisae magni vultumque recordor!*

(VIII, 155-6). The friendly relations between the rulers and the heroes' fathers are the bases for the present alliances and are the first things mentioned by the aged kings. Latinus thus expresses his familiarity with the history of Aeneas: *neque enim nescimus et urbem / et genus, auditique advertitis aequore cursum* (VII, 195-6). He refers to the hero's ancestor: *his ortus ut agris / Dardanus Idaeas Phrygiae penetravit ad urbes,* etc. (VII, 206 *ff.*) (4) The heroes with their companions are invited to partake of a feast. Compare the *Beowulf* 489-98 (Hrothgar's invitation and a description of the banquet) and VIII, 173-83 (Evander's invitation and an account of the feasting). The *Beowulf*-poet assumes that the Danes and the Geats had no difficulty in understanding each other's language: *Scop hwīlum sang / hādor on Heorote. Þǣr wæs hæleða drēam, / duguð unlýtel Dena ond Wedera* (496-8). Similarly Vergil describes the conversation of the Trojans and the Latins as he had described the spoken formalities of the Trojans and the Libyans in Book IV. (5) The heroes are said to be divinely sent. Hrothgar says of Beowulf, *Hine hālig God / for ārstafum ūs onsende* (381-2). So Latinus sees in the coming of Aeneas the fulfilment of divine prophecy: *Di nostra incepta secundent / auguriumque suum* (VII, 259-60); *Hunc illum poscere fata* (VII, 272). (6) The kings lament the decline of their youthful strength. Hrothgar's reminiscence is described thus: *hwīlum eft ongan eldo gebunden, / gomel gūðwiga gioguðe cwīðan, / hildestrengo; hreðer inne wēoll, / þonne hē wintrum frōd worn gemunde* (2111-14). Compare Evander's recollection of his youth: *O mihi praeteritos referat si Iuppiter annos, / qualis eram, cum primam aciem . . . / stravi,* etc. (VIII, 560 *ff.*), and his comment on his age: *Sed mihi tarda gelu saeclisque effeta senectus / invidet imperium seraeque ad fortia vires* (VIII, 508-9). (Compare also *sed enim gelidus tardante senecta / sanguis hebet frigentque effetae in corpore vires* (V, 395-6) with *eldo gebun-*

den, etc. (2111 *ff.*) and *bisgum gebunden* (1743). These phrases may be also noted: *aevo gravior* (II, 435); *fessum aetate* (II, 596); *confectum aetate* (IV, 599); *obsitus aevo* (VIII, 307); *aevo confectus* (XI, 85).) The introduction of the kings' remarks are similar: compare *gomela Scilding,* / *felafricgende feorran rehte* (2105-6) and *rex obsitus aevo* . . . / . . . *vario viam sermone levabat* (VIII, 307-9). (Compare also *Tum genitor, veterum volvens monumenta virorum* . . . / . . . *ait* (III, 102-3).) Hrothgar's remark to Beowulf as he confides to the Geat the keeping of Heorot is in tone with his other reference to his past strength: *Næfre ic ænegum men ær ālȳfde,* / *sipðan ic hond ond rond hebban mihte,* / *ðrȳpærn Dena būton þē nū ða* (655-7).

One Sacrificed for Many. The circumstances of the death of Hondscio are incongruous to the context of the Grendel-raid. It has been held[33] that the death of Beowulf's thane represents an old folk-tale survival in which the prowess of the all-conquering hero was exhibited only after other champions had been defeated. But this explanation has its difficulties: there is very little in the situation of the watchers in Heorot to have induced the *Beowulf*-poet to retain this legendary motif: in fact the situation is so unlike what we may imagine the older hero-tales to contain, that he would have every reason for discarding it. All the defenders of Heorot are asleep except Beowulf; if Hondscio were to represent the champion who first tried the monster's mettle, surely the poet would have allowed him to make some kind of a defense. It is difficult to imagine that the poet intended to emphasize Grendel's fierceness by having him kill in the presence of the watchful hero a defenceless sleeping man, his companion-in-arms. This is no place for the monster's fury to be displayed on weaker champions. His dreadful power is only too well known. Only the

---

[33] Lawrence, *Beowulf and Epic Tradition*, p. 176.

hero sent from God can avail against him. It is too illogical to think that the poet meant Hondscio's death to inspire Beowulf's ambition to succeed where a former warrior had failed. The inapplicability of the old heroic motif is too apparent here: we cannot imagine that the *Beowulf*-poet intended to force it into the situation at this point.

One may ask: How could the Geats fall asleep in such a place of danger? As soon as Hrothgar goes away, the poet remarks that the defenders betake themselves to slumber. Thus, illogically enough, all the Geats except the hero were at once put *hors de combat*. Hondscio's death is plainly a sacrifice. He is sacrificed to a malignant superhuman power, the power of darkness, and the fiends of hell. The gruesome details of his death (739-45) leave outstanding the impression of defence-less immolation.

Hondscio was doomed: in his report to Higelac, Beowulf states this with a conviction deeper than the passing comment of a narrator looking before and after upon the action he is relating: *Þær wæs Hondsciô hild onsæge, / feorhbealu fægum* (2076-7).

This idea of sacrifice is one of the deepest motifs in the *Aeneid*. It reappears in many different situations with its un-varying significance: the individual must be sacrificed to the higher good of the group. In accord with this imperious principle Aeneas is constantly brought to deny himself in the interests of his people: first, it refuses him the consolation of death in the burning city of Troy (II, 594-619); again, it takes him from the woman he loves, Dido, who perishes without reward because she defied the principle which Aeneas was bound to obey (IV, 265-76, 351-61; VI, 458-64); finally, it sends him forth alone to fight Turnus, who also represents the individual sacrificed in the interests of his people (XII, 183-94, 697 *ff.*).

Other characters in the *Aeneid* carry the rôle of the one sacrificed for the many: Iphigenia (II, 116); Sinon (II, 130-1—*assensere omnes et quae sibi quisque timebat / unius in miseri exitium conversa tulere*); Helen (II, 575-6—*subit ira cadentem / ulcisci patriam et sceleratas sumere poenas*,—thus Aeneas purposes her death); the helmsman of Orontes' boat (I, 115-16).

The clear statement of this principle occurs in V, 814-15; *Unus erit tantum, amissum quem gurgite quaeres; / unum pro multis dabitur caput.* This is prophetic of the death of Palinurus, foredoomed like Hondscio, one sacrificed for many.

As though the *Beowulf*-poet wished to repeat this motif, he represents Grendel's dam slaying Aeschere the night following Grendel's defeat. The ominous words *Sum sāre angeald / æfenræste* (1251-2) point to the impending sacrifice. Upon this occasion the poet takes Beowulf from the scene (1299-1301), as if, while intent upon repeating the sacrifice-idea, he wished to prevent the reproach of double remissness from falling upon the hero, who has had to remain an inactive witness of Hondscio's death. Hrothgar's lament *ic ne wāt hwæder / atol æse wlanc eftsīðas tēah* (1331-2) and Beowulf's remark to Higelac *Nōðer hȳ hine ne mōston . . . / bronde forbærnan, nē on bēl hladan* (2124-6) are reminiscent of Aeneas' grief for Palinurus: *nudus in ignota, Palinure, iacebis harena* (V, 871). This lack of funeral-rites is the reason of Palinurus' sorrow expressed to Aeneas in the Underworld (VI, 363-71).

The poet constantly comes back to the sacrifice-motif in describing the death of Beowulf. The aged hero goes forth against the dragon as a doomed victim, rather than as a warrior fighting in a fair field. He did not know the real cause of his death—the ancient curse (*seolfa ne cūðe, / þurh hwæt his worulde gedāl weorðan sceolde*, 3067-8). One may ask here: Why did not the curse affect the previous owners of the treasure? Beowulf is singled out for immolation, sacrificed to a malignant supernatural power, as were Hondscio, Aeschere, and Palinurus. The many premonitory hints of the poet prove that the sacrifice-idea was uppermost in his mind (see 2309-11, 2399-400, 2341-3, 2419-20, 2516-18). Beowulf feels the approach of his doom and takes leave of his comrades as if for the last time: *Gegrētte ðā gumena gehwylcne, / . . . hindeman sīðe* (2516-17). The poet makes him express his determination to go *alone* against the fire-drake: see his brave speech 2532-37 and Wiglaf's comments (*ðē hlāford ūs / þis ellenweorc āna āðōhte / tō gefremmanne,* 2642-4; *hē hyne sylfne gewræc / āna mid ecge,* 2875-6). In order to isolate Beowulf, the poet removes the thanes from the conflict by having them show the white feather in the face of danger. This extraordinary incident, so entirely out of keeping with Teutonic tradition, has been already discussed at some length.[33a] As an integral part of the poem, the desertion of the thanes is hard to account for; but the obvious necessity for this action is seen if we may regard the *Beowulf*-poet to be following out the Vergilian motif. Still, he cannot resist the feeling that the breach of tradition is too great to pass without comment: he puts into the mouth of Wiglaf these words: *Ic wāt geare, / þæt næron ealdgewyrht, þæt hē āna scyle / . . . gnorn þrōwian, / gesīgan æt sæcce* (2656-9). One believes that the poet would not have allowed Wiglaf to participate in the dragon-fight but for the fact that it was necessary for some successor to take charge of events following the hero's death, to provide for his funeral, and carry out his dying commands.

Beowulf feels that his death is a sacrifice to the good of his people; he rejoices that he has won for them a great treasure: *Ic ðāra frætwa Frēan ealles ðanc, / . . . þē ic hēr on starie, / þæs ðe ic mōste mīnum lēodum / ær swyltdæge swylc gestrȳnan* (2794-8).

[33a] See *ante*, pp. 29-30.

This lofty concept of sacrifice would have recommended itself with peculiar appositeness to such a man as we may imagine the *Beowulf*-poet to be: a writer schooled in the tradition of the Church. The Christian idea of self-sacrifice, and, more specifically, the idea of Christ's redemption find ready agreement with Vergil's *unum pro multis dabitur caput*.

Beowulf's Arrival at Denmark: Aeneas' Arrival at Libya. The description of Beowulf's coming to Denmark and his reception in Hrothgar's hall bears so many significant resemblances to Vergil's account of the landing of Aeneas in Libya, that one can hardly be satisfied in calling these parallels in situation mere accidental similarities. The heightening of the local color in the description of the hero's disbarkation and entertainment seemed to Gummere to suggest foreign influence of some kind; he comments thus: "The 'stone-gay' path from the sea to the palace, the courteous challenge of the strand-ward as Beowulf's ship comes to the shore, and the highly parliamentary answer of the chieftain,—these must be outward flourishes of the story added by the monkish poet who was fain to let some bit of southern color fall upon this passing sombre legend of the north."[34] A close examination of the two accounts of the arrival of the heroes and their entertainment will, it is believed, make plausible the assertion that the source of the "southern color" is the first book of the *Aeneid*. (1) Beowulf is accosted by the Danish sentry, who asks him before he allows him to proceed to explain the errand of his band of armor-bearers (*Hwæt syndon gē searohæbbendra?*, 237) and their origin (*Nū ic ēower sceal / frumcyn witan, ǣr gē fyr heonan / . . . furþur fēran*, 251-4). Aeneas and Achates are met by Venus in disguise, who asks them who they are (*Sed vos qui tandem?*, I, 369), whence they have come (*quibus aut venistis ab oris?*, I, 369), and whither they

[34] *Germanic Origins*, p. 103.

are going (*Quove tenetis iter?*, I, 370). (2) Beowulf makes reply readily, naming his origin (*Wē synt gumcynnes Gēata lēode*, 260) and his errand (*Wē þurh holdne hige hlāford þinne* / . . . *sēcean cwōmon*, 267-8), and refers with some pride to his personal ability (*Ic þæs Hrōðgār mæg* / *þurh rūmne sefan rǣd gelǣran*, 277-8). Aeneas (speaking also for his companion) says that they are Trojans (*Nos Troia antiqua* . . . / *Libycis tempestas appulit oris*, I, 375-7), states his errand (*Italiam quaero patriam et genus ab Iove summo*, I, 380), and boasts of his fame (*Sum pius Aeneas* . . . *fama super aethera notus*, I, 378-9). (3) Having satisfied their inquisitors, the newcomers are allowed to proceed. The Danish soldier says to Beowulf, *Gewītaþ forð beran* / *wǣpen ond gewǣdu* (291-2). He offers to guide him (*ic ēow wīsige*, 292), and promises additional protection (*swylce ic maguþegnas mīne hāte* / *wið fēonda gehwone flotan ēowerne,* / . . . *ārum healdan*, 293-6). Venus says to her son, *Perge modo, atque hinc te reginae ad limina perfer*, I, 389; *perge modo, et, qua te ducit via, derige gressum*, I, 401. The protecting cloud under which Venus sheltered Aeneas and his companions obviously could not be utilized by the Anglo-Saxon poet. By way of compensation, however, he allows the strand-guard to quit his station and lead the hero to the palace of the ruler. This seems to be out of keeping with the feeling of "preparedness" in the situation, for the sentry thus deserts an important post. His promises of additional security (293-6) agree with what Venus says to her son (*Quisquis es, haud, credo, invisus caelestibus auras* / *vitales carpis*, I, 387-8) and with the happy omen of the swans and the eagle (I, 393-400).

(4) The heroes then proceed toward the palaces of the rulers of the land. The path over which Beowulf and his men go is mentioned: *Strǣt wæs stānfāh* (320). Gummere remarks

that the street was "paved in the Roman fashion."[35] The Geats come in sight of their destination, the palace, which is described as very splendid (*Guman ōnetton, sigon ætsomne, oþ þæt hȳ sæl timbred / geatolīc ond goldfāh ongyton mihton; / þæt wæs foremǣrost foldbūendum / receda under roderum*, 306-10). Aeneas and his companion go to the city of Dido (*Corripuere viam interea qua semita monstrat*, I, 418); they come within view of Carthage (*Iamque ascendebant collem qui plurimus urbi / imminet adversasque aspectat desuper arces*, I, 419-20). Aeneas admires the road (*strata viarum*, I, 422) and the splendid buildings, particularly the brazen temple (I, 420-2, 446-93). (5) The heroes do not present themselves directly to the sovereigns but are introduced after several lengthy speeches by third parties. Beowulf and his troop are again stopped by Wulfgar, who, after parliamentary inquiry and reply, informs Hrothgar of the coming of the foreign warriors (331-99). The king hears of the hero's journey (*Hēr syndon geferede, feorran cumene / ofer geofenes begang Gēata lēode*, 361-2), and learns the hero's name (*þone yldestan ōretmecgas / Bēowulf nemnað*, 363-4). His favor is sought toward the newcomers (*nō ðū him wearne getēoh / ðīnra gegncwida, glædman Hrōðgār!*, 366-7). The king refers to the family and the reputation of the hero (372-81), is graciously disposed toward the hero in advance (*Ic þǣm gōdan sceal / for his mōdþræce mādmas bēodan*, 384-5), and expresses a desire to see him (*Bēo ðū on ofeste, hāt in gân / sēon sibbegedriht samod ætgædere; / gesaga him ēac wordum, þæt hīe sint wilcuman*, 386-8). Aeneas comes to Dido's attention through Ilioneus, who in a long speech informs her of the coming of the Trojans (I, 520-60). The queen learns of the hero's journey and hears his name (*Rex erat Aeneas nobis, quo iustior alter / nec pietate fuit nec bello maior et armis*, I, 544-

[35] *Germanic Origins*, p. 98.

5). She is asked to receive the Trojans with compassion (*Troes te miseri, ventis maria omnia vecti, / oramus: prohibe infandos a navibus ignes*, etc., I, 524 *ff*.). As Hrothgar is familiar with the events of Beowulf's life, so Dido knows of the labors of Aeneas and his followers (*Quis genus Aeneadum, quis Troiæ nesciat urbem / virtutesque virosque?* I, 565-6). She expresses her favor toward the hero (*Equidem per litora certos / dimittam et Libyae lustrare extrema iubebo, / si quibus eiectus silvis aut urbibus errat*, I, 576-8), and wishes to see him (*utinam rex ipse . . . afforet Aeneas*, I, 575-6).

(6) The heroes in coming before their royal hosts make a dramatic appearance. After the formal preliminaries Beowulf and his troop enter Hrothgar's presence. There is an evident attempt to make the entry of the hero as imposing as possible (*heaþorinc ēode / heard under helme, þæt hē on heorðe gestōd. / Bēowulf maðelode—on him byrne scān, / searonet seowed smiþes orþancum*, 403-6). In like manner the sudden appearance of Aeneas is described vividly. A part of the finely drawn details were of course inappropriate to the uses of the *Beowulf*-poet: *Restitit Aeneas, claraque in luce refulsit, / os umerosque deo similis; namque ipsa decoram caesariem nato genetrix lumenque iuventae / purpureum et laetos oculis afflarat honores* (I, 587-91). (7) Without invitation the heroes address the rulers. Beowulf begins his long speech to Hrothgar (407-55) with a self-introduction (*Ic eom Higelāces / mǣg ond magoðegn*, etc.). He tells of his former exploits, seemingly emphasizing the distress he suffered (*nearoþearfe drēah / . . . wēan āhsodon*, 422-3). (*Nearo* to the *Beowulf*-poet was an impressive word, which signified a feat of courage particularly difficult or painful. The word occurs but twice in the poem: it is used in line 2350 to refer to Beowulf's struggle with Grendel, and in line 2594 to refer to his fight with the fire-drake: *nearo ðrōwode / fȳre befongen*.) Implicit in Beo-

wulf's speech to Hrothgar is the idea that he is devoting himself to the Danish king in a spirit of entire allegiance. Aeneas
confronts Dido saying, *Coram, quem quaeritis, adsum, / Troïus
Aeneas* (I, 595-6). His speech to Dido (595-610) consists
chiefly of the story of his misfortunes (*nos, reliquias Danaum,
terraeque marisque / omnibus exhaustos iam casibus, omnium
egenos / urbe, domo socias . . . / Non opis est nostrae, Dido,
nec quidquid ubique est / gentis Dardaniae, magnum quae
sparsa per orbem,* I, 598-602). He promises unreserved allegiance to the queen (*semper honos nomenque tuum laudesque
manebunt / quae me cumque vocant terrae,* I, 609-10). (8) The
responses of the rulers refer to past events in the lives of the
ancestors of the heroes, and are an invitation to the newcomers
to share a regal feast. Instead of asking the questions which
Dido puts to the Trojans (*Quis te, nate dea, per tanta pericula
casus / insequitur? quae vis immanibus applicat oris?* I, 615-
16), Hrothgar makes the answers to them the beginning of his
reply to Beowulf: *For gewyrhtum þū, wine mīn Bēowulf, /
ond for ārstafum ūsic sōhtest* (457-8). The king goes on to
mention how he aided Beowulf's father, driven into exile (459-
72), at a time when he (Hrothgar) was a powerful ruler (*ðā ic
furþum wēold folce Deniga / ond on geogoðe hēold ginne
rīce, / hordburh hæleþa,* 465-7). He concludes his speech by
an invitation to a feast: *Site nū tō symle* (489). Having asked
the questions mentioned above, Dido inquires next about the
parents of Aeneas (*Tune ille Aeneas, quem Dardanio Anchisae / alma Venus . . . genuit?* I, 617-18). She recalls the
coming of the hero's proscribed ancestor to the domains of her
parents, who received the exile hospitably and gave him protection (*Atque equidem Teucrum memini Sidona venire /
finibus expulsum patriis, nova regna petentem / auxilio Beli,*
I, 619-21). Dido's parent, Belus, was then a powerful king
(*genitor tum Belus opimam / vastabat Cyprum et victor di-*

cione tenebat, I, 621-2). Lastly she invites Aeneas and his men
to a feast (*Quare agite, o, tectis, iuvenes, succedite nostris*,
I, 627). It is not inappropriate to remark that Dido's comment on her misfortune (*non ignara mali, miseris succurrere
disco*, I, 630) applies with peculiar appositeness to the present
state of Hrothgar's kingdom, and may find an echo in the
king's confession, *Sorh is mē tō secgan* . . . / . . . *hwæt mē
Grendel hafað* / . . . *færnīða gefremed* (473-6).He, too, is
not unacquainted with sorrows. (9) The visitors are seated in
the halls and are waited upon by servants. Beowulf and his
men take their places in Heorot (491-4), and are served by the
cup-bearer (*Þegn nytte behēold*, / *sē þe on handa bær hroden
ealowǣge*, / *scencte scīr wered*, 494-6). Similarly the Trojans
take their places in Dido's palace (*Iam pater Aeneas et iam
Troiana iuventus* / *conveniunt stratoque super discumbitur
ostro*, I, 699-700). The description of the serving-men is more
elaborate (I, 701-6). Mention is made of the Tyrian revelers
also (*Nec non et Tyrii* . . . *frequentes* / *convenere*, I, 707-
8); the *Beowulf*-poet refers to the presence of the Danes in
line 498.

Without any substantial change in order, these parallels
have been gathered from lines 237-498 of the *Beowulf*
and lines 369-707 of the first book of the *Aeneid*. The Unferth intermezzo begins abruptly with line 499, for which
there is no correspondence in Book I, but which has been
shown to have a close resemblance with a later episode in the
Aeneid, Book Eleven.[35a] There are in the following description
of the feast in the *Beowulf* several additional details which
seem to echo the story of the revels in the banquet-room of
Dido. The noise of merriment is described thus: *Ðǣr wæs
hæleþa hleahtor, hlyn swynsode*, / *word wǣron wynsume*
(611-12). Vergil mentions the sound of revelry (*Fit strepitus
tectis vocemque per ampla volutant* / *atria*, I, 725-6) and

[35a] See *ante*, pp. 106-10.

next describes the crowning honor of the feast: Dido's filling of the wine-crater,—*Hic regina gravem gemmis auroque poposcit / implevitque mero pateram*, (I, 728-9). The queen, Wealhtheow, performs a like ceremony in Hrothgar's feast (612 *ff.*). The queens present the cups to the highest noble of native birth: Hrothgar's queen gives him the cup first (*ond þā frēolīc wīf ful gesealde / ǣrest Ēast-Dena ēþelwearde*, 615-16); Dido presents it to her admiral Bitias (*tum Bitiae dedit*, I, 738). The action of the recipients is described: it is said of Hrothgar *hē on lust geþeah / symbel ond seleful* (618-19); Bitias is described thus: *ille impiger hausit / spumantem pateram* (I, 738-9). Lastly it is said that the other members of the company are served: *Ymbēode þā ides Helminga / duguþe ond geogoþe dǣl ǣghwylcne, / sincfato sealde* (620-2); compare *post, alii proceres* (I, 740). Wealhtheow's *sincfato* and the *wunderfatum* from which wine is poured (1162) may be Dido's *patera gravis gemmis auroque*. The wine and wonder-vats are certainly far removed from drinking-horns and real Germanic beer. The feast as a whole is too highly colored: there is too much courtliness and decorum about it. "The speech of Beowulf" (402-661) Gummere says, "is too parliamentary for the temper of those earliest Germans; and perhaps the queen herself is something too much of a *grande dame*." It may be asked: Did Hrothgar's courtly gold-decked queen owe any of her imperial manner to the hostess of Aeneas? Compare the fine personal description of Dido: *cui pharetra ex auro, crines nodantur in aurum / aurea purpuream subnectit fibula vestem*, etc. (IV, 138 *ff.*).

It may be mentioned further that during the feasts the heroes are called upon to relate their past exploits: Beowulf tells of his swimming-victory over Breca, and Aeneas recounts the story of the fall of Troy (*quorum pars magna fuit*) and his adventures by sea and land prior to his arrival at Libya. These speeches alike form the longest sections of transposed narrative in the epics, Beowulf's story (with Unferth's version) running from line 499 to 607, and Aeneas' story comprising the second and third Books of the *Aeneid*.

Closely connected with the parts of the poems which have been discussed, there are to be noted many other similarities in narrative and descriptive detail which should properly be examined with attention. These details combine to make up a representation of court life which can hardly be imagined as characteristic of northern Europe of the sixth century. It was a tendency common to the Anglo-Saxon poets to touch all descriptive passages with their own local color: e.g. the description of the banquet of Holofernes in *Judith*, where "the eldest of his thanes" revelled with his king. The Old English poet usually practised staging his scene in places familiar to him, rather than going abroad for details of setting. The opposite impression is gained in the *Beowulf*: the story is not of an English hero, and the description of the Danish court seems to transcend the limits of what we can conceive the hall of an early Teutonic ruler to be. One feels that the poet, dissatisfied with the simpler qualities of the life he knew, went abroad to discover and utilize in his epic many details of refinement and decoration, which can hardly be thought of as being the products of an unassisted imagination.

The Palace Heorot. Hrothgar's hall, contrary to the usual Germanic custom, is a building separate from the *burh* proper.[36] It is frequently referred to as the greatest hall under heaven (78, 310, 412), unlike any other known to men (309). It is decorated with gold (167, 715, 308, 1800, 1639, 1253, 2083) and golden tapestries hang on the walls (994). The word *goldsele* is found only in the *Beowulf*: it is used 4 times

[36] Gummere, *Germanic Origins*, p. 104.

in the poem, each time in reference to Heorot. (Gummere says of the tapestries that they were "of course no primitive adornment, though not necessarily late in the history of Germanic decoration.")[37] The lavish interior decoration of Heorot reminds one of Dido's hall (*At domus interior regali splendida luxu / instruitur mediisque parant convivia tectis*, etc., I, 638 *ff.*), especially when one notes the verbal similarity and the corresponding passive verb in this passage describing the adornment of Hrothgar's banquet hall: *Ðā wæs hāten hreþe Heort innanweard / folmum gefrætwod* (991-2). The abundance of gold in the *Beowulf* was one of Stjerna's chief reasons for supposing that the poem could not have been composed in England.[38] The light of this gold-decked hall shines over many lands (311). Its attributes were synonymous with the joys of life itself: it is called "ring-hall" (1177, 2010), "beer-hall" (482, 492), "lord-hall" (767, 485), "war-hall" (443), and "wine-hall" (771, 695). It is a sacred place: it has a holy-of-holies (168), which cannot be approached by an evil spirit. No weapons are allowed in it: Beowulf's men are ordered to stack their arms outside the door (397-8). When Grendel, the unclean guest, is slain, Heorot is said to be *cleansed* (1176, 432). Of the verb employed here (*fǣlsian*), Sarrazin says, "Das verbum 'faelsian' wider in guten zustand bringen 'reinigen' muss ein sacrale bedeutung gehabt haben."[39]

Heorot is the symbol of a great nation, one of the principal unifying motifs in the epic. It was built by the hands of the people it sheltered (68-9, 74-6); there they ate and slept (1013-14, 484-5, 118-19). Upon the description of this palace the poet has lavished all his skill; he attempts no similar portrayal of any other hall, even though he has to deal with

[37] *Germanic Origins*, p. 107.
[38] See *Essays on Beowulf*, p. 147, and Chambers' edition of *Beowulf*, pp. 348-9.
[39] *Anglia*, 19, p. 371.

the palace of the hero's king, and the hall of King Beowulf himself. Higelac's palace is merely referred to as *betlīc* and *heā* (1925-6); Beowulf's royal dwelling-place receives even scantier mention: the poet only calls it *hām, / bolda sēlest* (2325-6). The extra attention given to Heorot as a palace, not necessarily as the residence of Hrothgar, is worthy of special attention. It may be that the poet had in mind the Trojan palaces and the banquet-room of Dido. The reference to Troy offers a peculiarly tempting parallel. At the first mention of the completed palace of Hrothgar, one's mind is taken back to "Ilion's lofty temples robed in fire." Was the poet thinking of burning Troy when he wrote the ominous words *heaðowylma bād, / lāðan līges* (82-3)? The patriotic feeling which centers in Heorot has a memorable parallel in the love of the Trojans for their city. The fame of the city of Troy also spread over many lands; it was the center of all the affections of Trojans everywhere,—religious, social, political. Men prefer dying in its defense to leaving the city to its conquerors. Heorot, like Troy, is attacked at night by an ancient enemy, while those who should be guarding are asleep: [*Grendel*] *fand þā ðǣr inne æþelinga gedriht / swefan æfter symble* (118-19). This was the situation in Troy: *fusi per moenia Teucri / conticuere; sopor fessos complectitur artus* (II, 252-3). Why should the *Beowulf*-poet say next *sorge ne cūðon / wonsceaft wera*? Is it an echo of *Myrmidonum dolos* (I, 252)? So fixed in the poet's mind is the idea of the *sleeping defenders*, that he allows the Geats to fall asleep in the guarded hall which their leader has promised they shall defend upon their honor (688-90, 728-30). The sleep of the defenders is almost absurdly incongruous to the air of danger which the poet has expressed as known to them only too well (691-6). Again the hall-warders sleep when Grendel's mother returns (1251). Full sorely, says the poet ominously, did one of them pay for his rest in that hall which, like Troy, was *somno vinoque sepultam* (II, 265). These ominous forebodings which the *Beowulf*-poet mentions as known to the defenders (691-6) are not lacking in the *Aeneid*: Hector's spirit foretold the city's doom to Aeneas in a dream (II, 289-95). The sleep of the defenders of Heorot seems forced and grotesque, a motif which has no coherence with the foregoing movement of the narrative. It may be a badly handled borrowing from the *Aeneid*. Vergil, we know, employed it more than once: Nisus and Euryalus find the Latin camp in much the same condition as that of Troy: *Passim somno vinoque per herbam / corpora fusa vident* (IX, 316-17). (See also IX, 236-7, 189-90.) Vergil's use of words in describing these two scenes varies so slightly, that a reading of one scene would almost inevitably recall the other and would tend to make the recollection of the motif stand out clearly. Is it unnatural that the *Beowulf*-poet should attempt to introduce the idea of the fatal sleep into his epic, seeing that it was so dramatically employed by Vergil?

The elaborate formality with which the *Beowulf*-poet has described the negotiations between Hrothgar and his guest has been discussed in detail. The general impression received from the poet's description of the Danish court would make one believe that the ceremonies which regulate the order of the day in Heorot were indeed very much beyond what his observation could have afforded him. When Beowulf arrives in Denmark, even though the day is not a special one and the noble guest is unexpectedly announced, Hrothgar is sitting on his throne of state, surrounded by his liege-men, like a king giving a regular audience. So Dido first appears in the *Aeneid* (I, 495 *ff.*) seated on her throne and dispensing justice; so the Trojans find king Latinus (*intus templo divum patriaque Latinus / sede sedens*, VII, 192-3); they meet king Evander

under similar circumstances (*una omnes iuvenum primi pau-
perque senatus*, VIII, 105). Hrothgar never goes unaccom-
panied by his warriors: e.g. *cyning / . . . tryddode tīrfæst
getrume micle, / cystum gecȳþed, . . . / medostigge mæt
mægþa hōse* (920-4). Compare the description of the company which attends upon Dido: *Dido / incessit, magna iuvenum stipante caterva* (I, 496-7); *progreditur, magna stipante
caterva* (IV, 136).

The most noteworthy parallel remains to be mentioned:
the songs of the minstrels in the palace of Hrothgar and the
banquet room of Dido. The contents of the songs are given
in some detail, sufficient to show a resemblance so striking
that it can hardly be called fortuitous. This is the song of
Hrothgar's scop:

> *Sægde sē þe cūþe*
> *frumsceaft fīra feorran reccan,*
> *cwæð þæt se Ælmihtiga eorðan worhte,*
> *wlitebeorhtne wang, swā wæter bebūgeð,*
> *gesette sigehrēþig sunnan ond mōnan*
> *lēoman tō lēohte landbūendum,*
> *ond gefrætwade foldan scēatas*
> *leomum ond lēafum, līf ēac gesceōp*
> *cynna gehwylcum þāra ðe cwice hwyrfaþ.*—90-8.

Thus sang Dido's minstrel Iopas:

> *Cithara crinitus Iopas*
> *personat aurata, docuit quem maximus Atlas.*
> *Hic canit errantem lunam solisque labores;*
> *unde hominum genus et pecudes, unde imber et ignes;*
> *Arcturum pluviasque Hyadas geminosque Triones;*
> *quid tantum Oceano properent se tingere soles*
> *Hiberni vel quae tardis mora noctibus obstet.*—I, 740-6.

There seems to be more similarity between these songs than
between the recitation of Hrothgar's scop and Caedmon's

Hymn of the Creation, in which mention is made only of the creation of the heavens and the earth. The song of Iopas contains, like the scop's song, reference to the sun and moon, living beings, and seasonal changes. The tone of Caedmon's *Hymn*, being Christian, is of course much nearer to the scop's recitation; but the setting of the latter would call to mind rather the song of Iopas than the *Hymn* of Caedmon. It is conceivable that the poet knew the Anglo-Saxon hymn, and in his story of creation imitated its spirit, but was inspired in the first place by the fine scene from Vergil. The words of Anchises to Aeneas, (VI, 724-9) also afford an instructive parallel:

Principio caelum ac terras camposque liquentes
lucentemque globum lunae Titaniaque astra
spiritus intus alit, totamque infusa per artus
mens agitat molem et magno se corpore miscet.
Inde hominum pecudumque genus vitaeque volantum
et quae marmoreo fert monstra sub aequore pontus.

Bibliography

The following list contains the books and articles which have been used in the preparation of this study. For complete bibliographies the reader is referred to those compiled by Chambers (*Beowulf, An Introduction*, pp. 383-413) and Klaeber (edition of *Beowulf*, pp. cxxiii-clix). For the *Beowulf*, Klaeber's text has been followed, and the text of Paul Lejay for the *Aeneid*, with some minor variations in spelling. The latter furnishes a condensed bibliography (pp. lxxix-lxxxix).

GENERAL WORKS

A. C. CLARK,
   The Descent of Manuscripts. Oxford, 1918.
R. S. CONWAY,
   The Architecture of the Epic. London, 1925.
G. C. CRUMP and E. F. JACOBS, *Editors*,
   The Legacy of the Middle Ages. Oxford, 1926.
JOHN CLARK HALL,
   A Concise Anglo-Saxon Dictionary. New York, 1916.
WALTER MORRIS HART,
   Ballad and Epic. Boston, 1907.
MONTAGUE R. JAMES,
   The Wanderings and Homes of Manuscripts. New York, 1919.
W. P. KER,
   Epic and Romance. London, 1922.
JOHN EDWIN SANDYS,
   A History of Classical Scholarship. Cambridge, 1921.
EARNEST A. SAVAGE,
   Old English Libraries. London, 1911.
HENRY OSBORN TAYLOR,
   The Medieval Mind. New York, 1919.

REFERENCES FOR THE *BEOWULF*

The Unique Copy of the *Beowulf*, Vitellius A. XV. British Museum.
H. D'ARBOIS DE JUBAINVILLE,
   Littérature Celtique, Vol. I. Paris, 1883.

THOMAS ARNOLD,
  Notes on Beowulf. London, 1898.
ALLEN R. BENHAM,
  English Literature from Widsith *to the Death of Chaucer.* New
    Haven, 1916.
STOPFORD A. BROOKE,
  The History of Early English Literature. London, 1914.
MORGAN CALLAWAY, JR.,
  "The Appositive Participle in Anglo-Saxon," *Publications of the
    Modern Language Association*, 16, pp. 141-360.
H. M. CHADWICK,
  The Heroic Age. Cambridge, 1912.
  The Origin of the English Nation. Cambridge, 1924.
R. W. CHAMBERS,
  Beowulf, *An Introduction.* Cambridge, 1921.
  Widsith, *A Study in Old English Heroic Legend.* Cambridge, 1912.
  Beowulf, *with the* Finnsburg *Fragment*, revised edition of A. J.
    Wyatt. Cambridge, 1920.
ALBERT S. COOK,
  "The Possible Begetter of the Old English *Beowulf* and *Widsith*,"
    Connecticut Academy Studies, April, 1922.
  "Cynewulf's Part in our *Beowulf*," *Connecticut Academy Studies*,
    1925.
  "Beowulfian and Odyssean Voyages," *Connecticut Academy Studies*,
    1926.
J. WIGHT DUFF,
  Homer and Beowulf, *A Literary Parallel.* London, 1906.
ROBERT HUNTINGTON FLETCHER,
  "The Arthurian Material in the Chronicles, especially those of
    Great Britain and France," *Harvard Publications*, 1906.
HENRI GAIDOZ,
  Cûchulainn, Béowulf, et Hercule. Paris, 1921.
FRANCIS B. GUMMERE,
  The Oldest English Epic. New York, 1922.
  Germanic Origins. New York, 1892.
SIVERT N. HAGEN,
  "Classical Names and Stories in the *Beowulf*," *Modern Language
    Notes*, Vol. 19, pp. 65 *ff.*, 156 *ff.*

JAMES A. HARRISON and ROBERT SHARP,
   Edition of *Beowulf* and *The Fight at Finnsburh*. Boston, 1885.
D. HORNBURG,
   Die Composition des Beowulf. Metz, 1877.
WENTWORTH HUYSHE,
   Beowulf, *An Old English Epic*. Translation and Notes. London,
      1907.
DOUGLAS HYDE,
   A Literary History of Ireland. London, 1920.
JOHN MITCHELL KEMBLE,
   MS. notes in a copy of *Beowulf* which passed to him through Rask
      (whose notes are included) from Thorkelin. British Museum,
      1834.
CHARLES W. KENNEDY,
   The Caedmon Poems. London, 1916.
W. P. KER,
   The Dark Ages. New York, 1904.
FR. KLAEBER,
   Edition of *Beowulf*. New York, 1922.
   "Aeneis und Beowulf," *Archiv*, 126, pp. 40 *ff.*, 339 *ff.*
   "Die christlichen Elemente im Beowulf," *Anglia*, 35, pp. 111 ff.,
      249 *ff.*, 453 *ff.; Anglia*, 36, pp. 169 *ff.*
   "Beowulfiana," *Anglia*, 50, pp. 195 *ff.*
   "Studies in the Textual Interpretation of *Beowulf*," *Modern
      Philology*, III, pp. 235 *ff.*
WILLIAM W. LAWRENCE,
   Beowulf *and Epic Tradition*. Cambridge, 1928.
   "The Haunted Mere in *Beowulf*," *Publications of the Modern
      Language Association*, 27, pp. 208-45.
HENRY MORLEY,
   English Writers, Vol. I. London, 1887.
HUBERT PIERQUIN,
   Le Poème anglo-saxon de "Béowulf." Paris, 1912.
JAMES W. RANKIN,
   "A Study of the Kennings in Anglo-Saxon Poetry," *Journal of
      English and Germanic Philology*, VIII, pp. 357 *ff.*; IX, pp.
      49 *ff.*

JAMES EDWARD ROUTH,
>   *Two Studies on the Ballad Theory of the* Beowulf. Baltimore,
>   1905.
GREGOR SARRAZIN,
>   *Beowulf-Studien.* Berlin, 1888.
>   "Die Hirsch-Halle," *Anglia,* 19, pp. 368 *ff.*
W. J. SEDGEFIELD,
>   Edition of *Beowulf.* Manchester, 1910.
G. A. SMITHSON,
>   *The Old English Christian Epic.* Berkley, 1910.
KNUT STJERNA,
>   *Essays on Questions Connected with* Beowulf, trans. and ed. by
>   J. Clark Hall. London, 1912.
BERNHARD TEN BRINK,
>   *English Literature to Wiclif.* London, 1895.
BENJAMIN THORPE,
>   Beowulf: *Translation and Notes.* London, 1875.
CHAUNCEY B. TINKER,
>   *The Translations of* Beowulf. Yale Studies, 1903.
FREDERICK TUPPER,
>   *The Riddles of the Exeter Book,* New York, 1910.
BLANCHE COLTON WILLIAMS,
>   *Gnomic Poetry in Anglo-Saxon.* New York, 1914.
THOMAS WRIGHT,
>   *Biographia Britannica Literaria, Anglo-Saxon Period, Anglo-Norman
>   Period.* London, 1846.
A. J. WYATT,
>   Edition of *Beowulf.* Cambridge, 1898.
H. C. WYLD,
>   "Diction and Imagery in Anglo-Saxon Poetry," *English Associa-
>   tion Essays and Studies.* London, 1925.

REFERENCES FOR THE *AENEID*

MABEL L. ANDERSON,
>   *A Study of Vergil's Descriptions of Nature.* Boston, 1917.
FERNAND BAEDENSPERGER,
>   "Vergil's *Aeneid* and the Irish *Imrama:* Zimmer's Theory," *Mod-
>   ern Philology,* 15, pp. 449 *ff.*

H. M. BEATTY,
> *Dante and Virgil.* London, 1905.

ANDRÉ BELLESSORT,
> *Virgile, son œuvre et son temps.* Paris, 1927.

G. F. BROWNE,
> *The Venerable Bede.* London, 1919.

H. E. BUTLER,
> *The Sixth Book of the* Aeneid. Oxford, 1920.

REV. GEORGE CALDER,
> "The Irish Aeneid," *Publications of the Irish Texts Society.* London, 1907.

DOMENICO COMPARETTI,
> *Vergil in the Middle Ages*, trans. by E. F. M. Benecke. New York, 1895.

JOHN CONINGTON and HENRY NETTLESHIP,
> Edition of *P. Vergili Maronis Opera*, Vols. II and III. London, 1883, 1884.

M. M. CRUMP,
> *The Growth of the* Aeneid. Oxford, 1920.

WILLIAM WARDE FOWLER,
> *Virgil's Gathering of the Clans.* Oxford, 1918.
> *Aeneas at the Site of Rome.* Oxford, 1918.
> *The Death of Turnus: Observations on the Twelfth Book of the* Aeneid. Oxford, 1919.

TENNEY FRANK,
> *Vergil, A Biography.* New York, 1922.

C. J. B. GASKOIN,
> *Alcuin: His Life and Work.* London, 1904.

TERROT REAVELEY GLOVER,
> *Studies in Vergil.* London, 1904.

FRANCIS J. HOSFORD,
> "Virgil and the Transition from Ancient to Modern Literature," *Classical Journal*, Vol. 6, pp. 3 *ff.*

HENRY H. HOWORTH,
> *Saint Augustine of Canterbury.* New York, 1913.

PAUL LEJAY,
> Édition de *l'Énéide.* Paris, 1926.

WALLACE M. LINDSAY,
> *Ancient Lore in Medieval Latin Glossaries.* London, 1921.

O. M. Long,
   "The Attitude of Alcuin Toward Vergil," *Johns Hopkins Press*,
   Gildersleeve Studies. Baltimore, 1902.

Friedrich Lorentz,
   The Life of Alcuin, trans. by Jane M. Slee. London, 1837.

John MacInnes,
   "The Conception of *Fata* in the *Aeneid*," *Classical Review*, Vol.
   24, pp. 169 *ff*.

J. W. Mackail,
   Classical Studies. London, 1925.

Nicholas Moseley,
   Characters and Epithets—A Study in Vergil's Aeneid. London.
   1926.

H. Nettleship,
   Vergil. New York, 1880.

Elizabeth Nitchie,
   Virgil and the English Poets. New York, 1919.

M. B. Ogle,
   "Dame Gossip's Rôle in Epic and Drama," *American Philological
   Transactions*, Vol. 55, 1924, pp. 90 *ff*.

T. L. Papillon and A. E. Haigh,
   Edition of the *Aeneid*. Oxford, 1892.

M. Roger,
   L'Enseignement des Lettres Classiques d'Ausone à Alcuin. Paris,
   1905.

Thomas F. Royds,
   The Beasts, Birds, and Bees of Virgil. Oxford, 1918.

J. E. Sandys,
   A History of Classical Scholarship. Cambridge, 1921.

W. Y. Sellar,
   Roman Poets of the Augustan Age: Virgil. Oxford, 1883.

A. Sidgwick,
   Edition of *P. Vergili Maronis Opera*. Cambridge, 1894.

D. A. Slater,
   Sortes Vergilianae. Stratford, 1921.

Henry Osborn Taylor,
   The Classical Heritage of the Middle Ages. New York, 1901.

J. S. Tunison,
   Master Virgil. Cincinnati, 1890.

A. F. WEST,
   Alcuin and the Rise of the Christian Schools. New York, 1901.
MONROE NICHOLS WETMORE,
   Index Verborum Vergilianus. New Haven, 1911.
GEORG ZAPPERT,
   Virgils Fortleben im Mittelalter. Vienna, 1851.

Index